S0-ADN-716

PORTFOLIO

TATALOG

Currently a member of the Group Executive Council of Tata Sons, Harish Bhat has held many roles in the Tata Group over the past twenty-seven years, including managing director of Tata Global Beverages, and chief operating officer of the watches and jewellery businesses of the Titan Company Ltd.

Harish is an alumnus of BITS Pilani and Indian Institute of Management Ahmedabad. He won the IIMA gold medal for scholastic excellence, and later the British Chevening Scholarship for young managers. An avid marketeer, he has helped create many successful Tata brands. He writes extensively, and is a columnist for the *Hindu Business Line* and *Mint*.

Harish is an incorrigible foodie and fitness freak. His wife, Veena, is a professor of computer science. They have a teenage daughter, Gayatri. He can be reached at bhatharish@hotmail.com.

PRAISE FOR THE BOOK

'A sensitive insider and an old Tata hand . . . Bhat emerges a good storyteller in *Tatalog*. This is not purely a tome on management; it is neither just a work on corporate history. This is an attempt to capture the spirit (or the soul) of the Tatas. For the uninitiated, there is the revelation of the Tata Way'—*Businessworld*

'These are, of course, well-documented stories; yet, hearing them from a Tata insider gives one a glimpse into the decision-making processes of a massive conglomerate, and the considerations that drive them'—*Outlook Money*

'Every episode is narrated with passion and childlike excitement, touched with gentle humour. It sticks to the task of telling the stories straight and succeeds in holding our attention and interest all the way through'—*Deccan Herald*

'An interesting look into a group that has survived the vicissitudes of negotiating the tricky terrains of Indian business better than most'—*Business India*

TATA LOG

Eight Modern Stories from a Timeless Institution

HARISH BHAT

PORTFOLIO
PENGUIN

PORTFOLIO
Published by the Penguin Group
Penguin Books India Pvt. Ltd, 7th Floor, Infinity Tower C, DLF Cyber City,
Gurgaon 122 002, Haryana, India
Penguin Group (USA) Inc., 375 Hudson Street, New York, New York 10014, USA
Penguin Group (Canada), 90 Eglinton Avenue East, Suite 700, Toronto,
Ontario, M4P 2Y3, Canada
Penguin Books Ltd, 80 Strand, London WC2R 0RL, England
Penguin Ireland, 25 St Stephen's Green, Dublin 2, Ireland
(a division of Penguin Books Ltd)
Penguin Group (Australia), 707 Collins Street, Melbourne, Victoria 3008,
Australia Penguin Group (NZ), 67 Apollo Drive, Rosedale,
Auckland 0632, New Zealand
Penguin Books (South Africa) (Pty) Ltd, Block D, Rosebank Office Park,
181 Jan Smuts Avenue, Parktown North, Johannesburg 2193, South Africa

Penguin Books Ltd, Registered Offices: 80 Strand, London WC2R 0RL, England

First published in Portfolio by Penguin Books India 2012
This paperback edition published 2014

Copyright © Harish Bhat 2012

All rights reserved

10 9 8 7 6 5 4 3 2 1

The views and opinions expressed in this book are the author's own and the facts
are as reported by him which have been verified to the extent possible, and the
publishers are not in any way liable for the same.

ISBN 9780143423348

Typeset in Minion Regular by SÜRYA, New Delhi
Printed at Replika Press Pvt. Ltd, India

This book is sold subject to the condition that it shall not, by way of trade or
otherwise, be lent, resold, hired out, or otherwise circulated without the publisher's
prior written consent in any form of binding or cover other than that in which it is
published and without a similar condition including this condition being imposed
on the subsequent purchaser and without limiting the rights under copyright
reserved above, no part of this publication may be reproduced, stored in or
introduced into a retrieval system, or transmitted in any form or by any means
(electronic, mechanical, photocopying, recording or otherwise), without the prior
written permission of both the copyright owner and the above-mentioned publisher
of this book.

A PENGUIN RANDOM HOUSE COMPANY

*Dedicated to the late R.M. Lala, historian of the Tata Group
and chronicler of its personalities, traditions and culture*

Contents

Foreword   ix

Acknowledgements   xiii

A Path Well Paved   1

Tata Indica, the Very First Indian Car   20

Uplifting Tales from Okhamandal   50

The Tribulations of Tata Finance   69

Tanishq Sets the Gold Standard   82

Second Careers for Intelligent Women   105

EKA: Birth of an Indian Supercomputer   130

Tetley Enters the Tata Fold   150

Tata Steel Wins the Deming Prize   174

Epilogue: One Day in Kolkata   195

Foreword

I am delighted to write a foreword to *Tatalog*, this wonderful book by Harish Bhat. The idea of a Tata director writing the foreword to a Tata colleague's book on Tata might appear somewhat incestuous. So, why am I doing it?

I am writing this foreword not merely because Harish asked me to, but because I am fascinated by his work. He could have been a successful writer had he not become a business manager. He is a master storyteller. In the world of business, storytelling is not a skill that is particularly envied—the expression has pejorative undertones, and suggests tall tales and fiction rather than fact. But Harish's kind of storytelling actually plays a valuable role in business.

How do you assemble solid facts and incidents, often mundane when they occurred, into a narrative that interests the reader and leaves him or her with an overarching message? That is the art at the heart of corporate storytelling. And Harish does it very well.

Stories and narratives are at the heart of human evolution. Every region and society has its storytellers and related traditions: there are the Berbers of Jama'al Fina in Marakkech, the Harikatha speakers of Tamil Nadu and the Jatra performers of Bengal, not to forget the tradition of the troubadours, bards and minstrels in Europe. The stories accumulate and become modern symbols of a social community.

What would Egypt be without the story of Osiris, Greece without Prometheus or India without Vaishampayana's masterly dictation of the story of the *Mahabharata* to the scribe Ganapati? Stories and anecdotes have evolved and come to represent the distinctiveness of a society and the culture of its people.

In his celebrated book *The Hero with a Thousand Faces*, the mythologist Joseph Campbell expounded the startling theory of the monomyth, showing that ancient stories from around the world are based on a standard structure and are made up of similar elements. Campbell identified seventeen stages in the development of all stories, and categorized these into three sections: the hero's Departure, Initiation and Return.

- Departure involves a hero venturing forth from a common world into a supernatural world, e.g. Rama's departure into Dandakaranya.
- Initiation details the myriad challenges faced by the hero, which he overcomes to emerge victorious, e.g. Rama's travails in the forest and in Lanka.
- Return deals with the hero coming back from his mysterious adventures with great and newly acquired powers to benefit other people, e.g. Rama's triumphal return to Ayodhya and his coronation.

You can see the same pattern in every legendary story from every land: Yudhisthira, Ulysses, Gautama Buddha. The same patterns appear in the historical stories of the world wars and the colonization and subsequent independence of India. So why would they not apply to the story of a corporation?

Harish has deployed these principles and concepts in an impressive way. He has done so with what one could consider fairly mundane events that were encountered by a company!

However, the organization happens to be a long-living corporation—which Harish refers to as a 'timeless institution'.

The Tata organization began almost one and a half centuries ago, and has had only four chairmen before Ratan Tata. Since the average life of *Fortune 500* companies is under forty years, the very fact of long-lived and calibrated continuity makes Tata an interesting subject of study.

Is there a secret sauce to its long life? How did it change and adapt from the Victorian era to the information era? In his celebrated book about long-life companies, *The Living Company*, author Arie de Geus identified four Ds that are key to longevity:

- Developing an intense sensitivity to the environment
- Displaying a cohesive purpose and identity
- Demonstrating tolerance to diverse views
- Deploying finance conservatively

Perhaps many—or all—of these characteristics apply to Tata.

Many of the early stories of Tata have been memorably captured by Russi Lala in his widely read and masterful books *The Creation of Wealth* and *For the Love of India*. Lala narrated stories about Jamsetji Tata's dogged determination to envision and execute nationally relevant projects. There was restlessness in the founder, who desperately wanted to build human capabilities through education and science. He and his successors persisted with public advocacy to do what is right for the nation as expressed through the encounters with Lord Curzon and Pandit Nehru and, lastly, collaborated after Independence with other industry doyens of the time to write the Bombay Plan.

Several Tata directors provided public service leadership: Ghulam Mohammed became the first finance minister of

Pakistan, John Mathai became the second finance minister of India and Nani Palkivala became the de facto Indian 'finance minister'—though he never formally became one. Their examples are inspiring.

What Harish has captured is a subaltern's view of the post-liberalization decades from 1991 to date. He writes with candour about dreams, challenges, dilemmas, failures and successes. The dogged persistence reflected in the Tata Indica story, the recovery from the depths of the Tata Finance debacle, the imaginative development of the EKA (which was most likely the world's first privately funded supercomputer)—all these and many more appear in the pages of this book. All of these are told with the formula of Departure, Initiation and Return of the hero, who in this case is a corporation rather than a person.

Tatalog is commendable as a work of corporate history through storytelling, as a personal view of history and, finally, as an act of love for a 'timeless institution'.

Mumbai   R. GOPALAKRISHNAN
26 September 2012

Acknowledgements

The Tata Group has been the inspiration for this book. This is the foremost acknowledgement I wish to record.

I would like to thank the Tata Group and Ratan Tata, chairman, Tata Sons, for the opportunity to undertake this project and document these memorable stories. I would, however, like to clarify that many of the opinions expressed in these pages are my personal views and may not necessarily be the views of the Tata organizations and people who are featured.

My sincere thanks to Bhaskar Bhat, managing director of Titan Industries, with whom I first broached the subject of writing this book, during the time I was heading the watches business in that company. This was an unusual proposal from a senior manager in his team, but he was spontaneously supportive.

R.K. Krishna Kumar, vice-chairman of Tata Global Beverages and director of Tata Sons, provided me with constant encouragement and several insightful perspectives about the Tata Group that have helped me think deeply about what constitutes the Tata Way.

R. Gopalakrishnan, executive director of Tata Sons, and a reputed author in his own right, kindly agreed to be my mentor in this voyage of creation. The discussions with him were always very engaging and insightful, and I came out of every such meeting with several new ideas, many of which have honed and sharpened the theme of this book. He gave generously of his time and also consented to write the foreword.

Christabelle Noronha, Chief, Group Publications at Tata Sons and an excellent writer, has been a friend, philosopher, critic and guide. Her advice and her support at every step of this journey have been invaluable. Whenever I ran into a stumbling block, I promptly ran into her office for help. She also opened many doors that I had never known of earlier.

This book has only been possible because of the extensive help and access I have received from more than a hundred people within several Tata companies. This includes senior directors and managers, people on the shop floors, former employees and associates. You will meet many of them individually in the pages of this book, so I have chosen not mention their names here. They narrated to me the wonderful and endearing stories that are the essence of this book. They accompanied and introduced me to the locations where these tales are set. They were patient with me, even as they reached deep into their memories to bring up recollections of people and episodes from current and distant history. I say to all of them, these are your stories, thank you for sharing them with me and giving me the privilege of penning them down.

I would also like to acknowledge the help and inputs of many people outside the Tata Group who shared their perspectives on some of the stories. Many of them had followed these stories closely and others had been participants themselves. They are also mentioned in these pages.

The Tata Management Training Centre, Pune, lent me its facilities for research, thinking and writing. Thanks are due to Chetan Tolia, the director of TMTC at that time, to many members of the faculty and staff of TMTC and to Sumandita Bora, librarian at TMTC, who provided me research assistance in several areas. There is a small desk and table in one corner of this library where I did much of the writing. TMTC is a beautiful, quiet place of knowledge, and I can think of no better place for creative contemplation.

A first-time author always awaits a publisher's response to his manuscript with anticipation and dread. Udayan Mitra of Penguin read the first few chapters of this book and decided within a few hours that it was worthy of publication. That was such a quick and positive response; I was doubly delighted.

To Anish Chandy, my editor, I will always be indebted. He has invested several hundred hours of personal effort in whipping this book into shape. He had to deal firmly with the enthusiastic but sometimes rambling labours of a rookie writer. Yet he did so in a very capable manner, wielding his digital red pencil to great effect. His editing prowess is fully matched by his powers of persuasion, and, as our conversations progressed each weekend, I felt the book being gradually but surely moulded in his expert hands.

Ameya Nagarajan, my copy editor, displayed remarkable patience in perfecting the text. Her meticulous edits and attention to detail put the finishing touches on this book.

Finally, I would like to acknowledge the role of three women in my life, who helped out in innumerable ways during the writing of this book.

My mother, Jayanthi, would constantly inquire about the progress of the book and tracked the whole effort silently from beginning to end. Her blessings were always a source of strength; they inspired the flow of my writing and helped deal with the writer's block that struck me from time to time.

My teenage daughter, Gayatri, read a few chapters and commented on them with an editor's alacrity, claiming that authority because she was editor of her school magazine.

My wife, Veena, participated in the writing of the book in so many different ways. She urged me to embark on the writing and to take a brief sabbatical from work for this purpose. She was the first person to read every chapter and would respond with her views immediately. On our frequent walks in the Krishna Rao Park in Bangalore, we would discuss some of these stories as they evolved, which helped me reflect on and refine the drafts. She provided me the constant encouragement and significant space required to address the rather lonely task of writing. Her spirited encouragement and companionship were the strong foundations on which this book was built.

I thank God Almighty for granting me the capability and resolve to write this book. I seek at His feet the gifts of knowledge and art that are the source of all creative effort.

A Path Well Paved

'It is not getting to the top of Everest that matters in life. It is how and why you get there.'

—Lord Hunt, who led the first successful
expedition to Mount Everest

Ratan Tata talks about a voyage

You can hear a pin drop when stories of great voyages are narrated by the captain of the ship. Ratan Tata, chairman of the Tata Group of companies, stood up to speak at the Crystal Room in the Taj Mahal Palace Hotel in Mumbai in February 2012. Over a hundred senior Tata managers eagerly listened to him describe how the Tata Group had achieved its revenue target of US$100 billion in 2011, up tenfold from US$10 billion in 2002. This made it the largest Indian enterprise, well ahead of the other industrial groups in the country. Amazingly, 60 per cent of group revenues were now derived from markets situated beyond India's borders, signifying the global spread of the Tata Group. It had also become one of the most visible conglomerates in the world, with over ninety companies engaged in widely different businesses ranging from salt to wristwatches to cars.

The managers listened with rapt attention as Ratan Tata highlighted some of the notable achievements of the Tata

Group over the past few years. It was a list that promised to make any corporate entity blush with pride. It had path-breaking innovations, such as the Nano car and the low-cost Tata Swach water purifier. Then came the gigantic global acquisitions like Corus, Jaguar, Land Rover and Tetley. Ratan Tata also mentioned India's largest information technology (IT) company, Tata Consultancy Services (TCS), and a clutch of companies that formed the country's second largest organized retailing business. Early moves in new-age sectors such as aerospace and financial services were showcased. Looking ahead, there was brief mention of the establishment of a new Tata Medical Centre and Cancer Hospital in Kolkata, at a substantial investment of US$70 million.

He ended his address with: 'Think big. Lead. Never follow.'

This was the last time Ratan Tata would speak as chairman at the Annual Group Management Meeting of the Tata Group. Twenty-one years earlier, in March 1991, the legendary J.R.D. Tata had stepped down as chairman of the Tata Group. He had personally selected Ratan Tata to lead the group into the twenty-first century. In December 2012, on reaching the retirement age of seventy-five years, Ratan Tata would hand over his role to forty-three-year-old Cyrus Mistry, who had been selected as his successor by the board of Tata Sons. Introducing Cyrus Mistry, Ratan Tata told his managers:

> Don't be fooled by his quiet demeanour. He is his own person, knows where he wants to be. I feel confident that he will lead the group in a manner that is of the highest integrity. Cyrus is the right person for the job; I welcome him.

150 years of the Tata Group

Over 150 years ago, in 1868, the founder and first chairman, Jamsetji Nusserwanji Tata, established a private trading firm in Bombay that has since grown and transformed into the mighty Tata Group.

Since those early days, the Tata Group has always been a strong catalyst in developing several sectors of India's economy. It established India's first steel plant at Jamshedpur, a company that is today a shining beacon in India's economic and social landscape. It opened the country's first luxury hotel, the Taj Mahal Palace, of which the Hollywood star Gregory Peck once said, 'The old Taj is the same—like a jewelled crown.' The Tata Electric Companies supply power with clockwork efficiency to India's economic capital, Mumbai. J.R.D. Tata's favourite venture was Tata Airlines, India's first airline company, which was later nationalized by the Central government. Tata Chemicals makes soda ash and salt in one of the most arid regions of the country, Okhamandal in Gujarat. Tata Global Beverages is one of the world's largest tea and coffee companies.

This voyage includes many other milestones in the non-profit sector. In 1892, the J.N. Tata Endowment for Higher Education, one of the world's first charitable trusts, was set up. This was an early effort at supporting the education of Indian students. The coveted scholarships provided by this trust have funded the studies of eminent scientists, jurists, economists and also a President of India. In 1912, for the first time in history of the world, the Tatas also instituted an eight-hour workday.

The Tata Group created several pioneering institutions, the list of which reads like a virtual roll call of some of the finest in the country today. The Indian Institute of Science, the Tata Institute of Social Sciences, Tata Memorial Hospital, the Tata Institute of Fundamental Research and the National Centre for the Performing Arts. While delivering all these to the nation and community, the Tata organization has simultaneously achieved unparalleled growth and prosperity for its shareholders. Annual profits for the year under review stood at a healthy US$7 billion, despite winds of recession in many parts of the world.

In addition, the Tata Group has continued to earn respect as a professionally managed enterprise fully committed to ethical values. The occasional aberrations do occur, and sometimes industry observers and the general public have been quite critical of such instances, particularly since the Tata Group is widely viewed as the gold standard for ethical conduct. Many employees of Tata, including this author, feel privileged to belong to an organization that has had a strong and positive impact on India and the world. There is a vivid sense of being part of a mission that stretches well beyond business. The Tata brand enjoys instant recognition and trust across households in India. It features prominently in global rankings for brand recall and respect. In 2012, the independent consulting firm Brand Finance listed Tata as a global Top 50 brand.

So, here is an enterprise that has not merely survived, but has flourished and grown from strength to strength over 150 years. The influential thinker and author Arie De Geus, in his excellent book *The Living Company*, has pointed out that the average life expectancy of a large multinational company— that is, companies that are listed in *Fortune 500* or its equivalent—is between forty and fifty years. Smaller companies that were surveyed in a few countries lasted for an average of twelve and a half years. Very few last for a century. By any of these standards, 150 years has been an extraordinarily long journey.

Such a voyage would have been nigh impossible if the path had not been well paved.

Is there a Tata Way?

This well-paved path is often loosely referred to in India, and also sometimes by global observers, as 'the Tata Way'. Is there a unique formula or secret sauce that the Tata Group has developed in its business laboratories that has led to its sustained success on so many fronts? If such a concoction exists, I'm sure several corporate chemists (and a host of aspiring alchemists) would be keen to know its magical ingredients.

However, such a bottled formula is not available for immediate consumption. What we do have is evidence of beliefs and behaviours in the Tata Group over a very long period of time. There have been letters composed, speeches delivered and books written. Some of these provide sharp insights into the Tata Way. Here are a few instances.

In 1895, at the opening of an extension of Empress Mills, Jamsetji Tata, chairman of the Tata Group, said:

> We do not claim to be more unselfish, more generous or more philanthropic than other people. But we think we started on sound and straightforward business principles, considering the interests of shareholders our own, and the health and welfare of the employees the sure foundation of our prosperity.

In 1965, J.R.D. Tata wrote to a Calcutta educationist: 'No success or achievement in material terms is worthwhile unless it serves the needs or interests of the country and its people, and is achieved by fair and honest means.'

In 2001, addressing an Annual Business Excellence Awards event of the Tata Group (also called the JRD-QV Awards night, where QV stands for Quality Value, and traditionally held on J.R.D. Tata's birthday, on 29 July), Ratan Tata spoke:

> The Tata Group must lead India in terms of what it does, not only in business but also as a corporate citizen and as a

participant in the country's growth. This is a holistic view. We want our managers and companies to drive their businesses using every means they can to achieve their ends, but they must do it in a way which stands out and continues the traditions that the group has established over the years.

You have aberrations from time to time. There is no perfect world. It is how we react to those aberrations and how we overcome those issues that will set us apart from the rest.

Reflections by other senior managers of the Tata Group are equally educative. I quote R. Gopalakrishnan, executive director, Tata Sons, in conversation with Ann Graham of the Conscious Capitalism Institute: 'We are hard-nosed business guys who like to earn an extra buck as much as the next guy, because we know that extra buck will go back to wipe away a tear somewhere.'

If the Tata Way is handed over to future generations through important legacies, then here is a perspective from R.K. Krishna Kumar, director of Tata Sons: 'I believe our real legacy is the great Tata trusts which own the group. They are like a sacred covenant.'

Stories of the modern age

While these views provide wise insight and sharp direction, an excellent method of understanding the Tata Way is to immerse oneself, with a curious and open mind, in some of the simple but powerful stories that embody this metaphor. These are interesting and gripping tales in their own right, but they are also opportunities for reflection on the themes that lie deep within.

Stories from the contemporary era also let us think about the Tata Way. Does it remain well paved and resilient even after so many decades of wear and tear, or has it become a bumpy, potholed road? These stories have been carefully chosen because they are distinctive enough to reveal the Tata Way of life.

- How Tata Motors went about making India's first indigenously designed car, the Indica
- How Tata Chemicals is transforming the lives of a community in a far-flung, semi-arid corner of the country
- The tale of Tanishq, and how Titan Industries is modernizing and transforming the huge jewellery industry in India
- The tribulations faced by Tata Finance, an episode that brought out the worst and the best in the organization
- How the Tata Second Career Programme gave women the opportunity and flexibility to re-enter the workforce
- The courage and conviction of the Tata Group that went into building the world's fourth fastest and Asia's fastest supercomputer
- The story of the first-ever acquisition of an iconic global brand by an Indian company—Tetley
- How a 100-year-old company, Tata Steel, became the first Indian organization to win Japan's prestigious Deming Prize for quality

All these stories belong to the period after 1992, when the Indian economy first began walking the road to liberalization. This was a time when many structures of the industrial licence era were dismantled, and fierce competition replaced rigid regulation in many business sectors. It was also the period when Ratan Tata became chairman and began charting the course for the future of the Tata Group.

There are a number of stunning tales that are not recounted in this book because they have already been covered extensively in the mainstream media. You will not find in these pages the story of the Tata Nano, also known as the people's car, the tale of the Taj Mahal Hotel in Mumbai, its employees and the extraordinary response to the unfortunate terrorist attacks on 26 November 2008 or the splendid story of TCS, India's flagship IT company.

Some other stories are still developing in the marketplace, and deserve to be told in their fullness at a later time. These include the foray into telecommunications, including the corporate lobbying and other controversies that dogged the Tata Group in this sector during 2010, and the gigantic acquisitions of Corus during 2007 and Jaguar Land Rover during 2008, both of which occurred several years after the Tetley deal.

What do the stories reveal?

As I went about researching these contemporary stories, they began to reinforce some well-known hypotheses of what the Tata Way was all about. A few interesting new insights also emerged. This learning was primarily the result of talking to the people who had participated in these stories, understanding their urges and experiences, their view of the people at the helm and also what drove their actions. It was also the result of visiting these locations across the country and sensing their energy, of extensive discussion and reading. It was by no means a statistically valid study, but, borrowing the terminology of the modern market researcher, it was dipstick qualitative research.

Four distinguishing characteristics emerged that clearly mark out the Tata Way. I call these the four Ps: **P**ioneering, **P**urposive, **P**rincipled and **P**erfect. The first three Ps are essential ingredients which have gone into paving the path. The fourth

P, however, is quite different. It emphasizes what the path is not. In order to grasp the Tata Way, it is important that these four characteristics are viewed as a collective.

The Tata Group is a PIONEERING organization

The word 'pioneer' refers to a person or a group that originates or helps to open up a new line of thought or activity. The Tata Group has demonstrated this repeatedly. In fact, the urge to be a pioneer appears to be a natural calling for Tata, well established over several generations.

A quick glance through India's corporate history will reveal that the Tata Group, in the early days of its founder Jamsetji Tata, pioneered steel manufacturing, luxury hotels and hydroelectric power generation in India. It is also widely known that the Tatas, during the time of J.R.D. Tata, pioneered aviation and India's first offshored IT company.

The liberalization of India's economy did not curtail this spirit of going where no Indian corporate had gone before. In the past two decades the Tatas have continued to be active pioneers in many more areas, taking large risks. Three stories in this book illustrate this theme.

The Tata Indica, India's first indigenously designed car, launched in 1998, is a sterling example. The fascinating story of how this car was made in a developing country with little existing infrastructure demonstrates the hunger and drive for charting a new course. When Ratan Tata was asked to speak about the Indica, he ended his speech with the words: 'All we know is that we thought of it, and we did it—we produced India's first car.'

Tanishq, India's first major jewellery brand, was launched in 1996. It has created the market for branded jewellery in India, and is well on its way to transforming this highly fragmented industry. Xerxes Desai, a career Tata man, founder of Titan Industries and creator of Tanishq, stood by this new idea despite initial resistance from some key members of the Tata Group. They thought it would never succeed. He was however provided latitude to propel the business, which is of course very successful today. Years later, the Tata Group would salute this pioneering venture. Xerxes Desai says that the excitement of being a pioneer can never be matched.

The Tetley acquisition was a pioneering effort because of three different reasons: it was the Tata Group's first large global purchase; it was the first time an Indian company was acquiring a significant brand, an intangible asset, rather than hard assets such as factories; it was the first leveraged buyout (LBO) acquisition by any Indian corporate entity. R.K. Krishna Kumar, vice chairman of Tata Global Beverages (known as Tata Tea at the time), who led this acquisition alongside Ratan Tata, maintains that it was a defining moment for the business, for the Tata Group and for India. He says that such moments come rarely in the lifetime of an organization and, when they do, pioneers seize them gladly.

There have also been many other pioneering and bold ventures during this period, all of them 'firsts' in their own right. However, only a select few have been covered in the book, including Asia's fastest supercomputer, built by Computational Research Laboratories (CRL), (2007), and Tata Steel winning the Deming Prize (2008).

The pioneering drive is as high today as it was in Jamsetji Tata's time, and there appears to be no sign of fatigue. Why?

The pioneering spirit is fed by vision, passion, courage and tenacity. It needs a bold and innovative approach. As some of the stories in this book demonstrate, the Tatas appear to have cultivated and nurtured these attributes in fair measure at various levels of the organization. What was the philosophy of the group's founder has become a way of life. Since the Tata Group is a diversified conglomerate, the ability to quickly learn from these pioneering practices across industries can also amplify their impact. For example, the experience of one global acquisition can help greatly in the next. This learning is particularly valuable when entering new areas, which is at the heart of pioneering.

The pioneering spirit has built for the Tata Group great new businesses that have become very prosperous. Such extraordinary success has further fuelled the urge to be prime movers. If the Tatas had not ventured boldly into creating India's first offshored IT company in 1968, well before the rest of India had even begun thinking of this industry seriously, TCS would never have scaled the IT summit.

A great pioneering organization needs men of enterprise, with a sense of destiny, at the helm of its affairs. Jamsetji Tata, the founder, was such a man, often compared to Rockefeller, Krupp and Ford. He set the pace, and the baton has been passed down for over a century now. Ratan Tata has demonstrated the same boldness of approach—in a 2006 interview he spoke of how he views risk as an ability to be where no one has been before. Chairmen with a grand vision have to be backed by equally bold and visionary men who believe in the vision, then strategize and execute it. The Tata Group has been most fortunate in this respect as well.

The Tata Group is a PURPOSIVE organization

To be 'purposive' is to be energized by a higher purpose that goes well beyond the narrow economic goals of growth or profit maximization.

All good business enterprises will be driven by economic goals, and they will thus meet the Nobel laureate Milton Friedman's expectation that 'there is one and only one social responsibility of business—to use its resources and engage in activities designed to increase its profits, so long as it stays within the rules of the game'.

Thankfully, the Tata Group has never agreed with Friedman's point of view. A key purpose of its existence, which has been clearly articulated, is to improve the quality of life in all the communities it serves. Indeed, it can be argued that the organization was never established to pursue economic objectives alone. Jamsetji Tata dreamt of an industrialized and prosperous India. This was the fundamental purpose with which he pursued business. Profits were very important, but so was the purpose. He chose to invest in steel, electric power and technical education, because he thought these three areas were critical for the country's progress at the time. Sir Stanley Reed, in his introductory notes to a biography of Jamsetji Tata, calls him a business patriot in the full sense of the term.

Purposiveness has remained a strong hallmark of the Tata Group in modern times. This is marked by an unwavering approach of putting the nation and the community at the heart of its activities. R. Gopalakrishnan, executive director, Tata Sons, says, 'We may be among the few companies around the world who think and act first as a citizen.' He recalls that when he joined the Tata Group, he was amazed at the inordinate amount of time and energy that senior directors dedicated to matters of the community and social responsibility. But he soon realized that this was the essence of the group's existence.

It is important to distinguish purposive behaviour from the desire to satisfy the needs of various stakeholders in a business, which many companies undertake today, and which is an admirable practice in its own right. Purpose is established and pursued independent of the needs of the business. It is broad in its definition, and often plays out at a much higher plane than the business itself. Nation building, community skilling and environment protection are noble purposes. On the other hand, ensuring that employees' children are provided good schooling or that customers are given excellent quality of products is not bracketed in the same league as purposive action.

Two interesting stories in this book bring out the purposive character of the Tata Group.

The creation of the Second Career Internship Programme (called SCIP) for qualified and experienced women who have taken breaks in their careers, mostly after becoming mothers, is a fascinating tale. This unique programme was created by the Tata Group's human resources team. Its objective is to provide these intelligent and skilled women with a bridge back to the workplace, and to ensure that their skills can be leveraged by the nation. The Tata Group invested significant resources and backed this idea with total commitment, despite not gaining anything in the short term. This has clearly been prompted by a higher purpose. The response from women in the target group has been extraordinary, showing that SCIP has touched a chord. Such programmes, when their full impact is felt, may well transform the possibilities of the workforce for India.

In a very different space, a small but creative business venture called Okhai has provided sustainable jobs and incomes to tribal women. A few years ago, as part of its vibrant community initiatives, Tata Chemicals established this beautiful handicrafts brand in the Okhamandal region of Gujarat, where the semi-arid environment has led to rather bleak lives. The company not only supplied people with the required facilities but also arranged for training by skilled designers and the best fashion technology institutes. The venture has transformed the lives of these local women. They are now so confident of their capabilities and buoyed by their success that they want to make Okhai the finest handicrafts brand across the world!

Virtually every large Tata company I know has demonstrated similar patterns of behaviour, though the extent of progress has varied widely. The stories of Tata trusts are also central to this narrative and, while they are not part of this book, they are brilliantly brought to life in the writings of the author and business historian R.M. Lala. These trusts own 66 per cent of Tata Sons (the holding company of the Tata Group) and support cherished institutions as well as large causes in areas such as literacy, prenatal care, education and health.

One thread running through the purposive behaviour of the organization over so many years has been a commitment to the country that its business is situated in—historically India, but in the future this could be anywhere. These words, written by Ratan Tata in 2009, could well have been written by the founder Jamsetji Tata a century ago: 'India is still a developing country, one burdened with enormous disparities. It is our duty to play whatever role we can, in whichever way we can, to diminish those disparities. This is the guiding principle for all of us at Tata.'

The Tata Group is a PRINCIPLED organization

When are companies entitled to call themselves principled? Technically, all organizations, including the Sicilian Mafia, can claim that they live by their coveted set of principles. However, if viewed in an appropriate context, I believe they earn this right when they act in accordance with morality, and

show a clear recognition of right and wrong in everything that
they do.

By this simple yardstick, the Tata Group has done well. It
has genuinely believed in the principles of integrity, honesty,
trust, caring and transparency. It has ensured consistent practice
of these principles. It has done this despite being rooted in
India, where corrupt practices are widespread. On the few
occasions that there has been a lapse in a Tata company's adherence
to the group's principles, the organization has admitted its
mistakes and dealt with them firmly and honourably.

This adherence to a principled approach has been reflected
in each generation of the Tata Group, making it such an
integral part of the Tata Way. Consider these expressions.

For the founder Jamsetji Tata, the 'ends' of entrepreneurial
success were always secondary to the 'means' by which they
were achieved.

J.R.D. Tata once wrote: 'I have often come to the conclusion
that if we were like other groups, we would be twice as big as
we are today. What we have sacrificed is a 100 per cent growth,
but we wouldn't want it any other way.'

Ratan Tata said in an interview:

> Business, as I have seen it, places great demand on you. It
> needs you to impose a framework of ethics, values, fairness
> and objectivity on yourself at all times. It is easy not to do this;
> you cannot impose it forcibly because it has to become an
> integral part of you. What has to go through your mind at the
> time of every decision, or most decisions, is does this stand the
> test of public scrutiny . . . ? As you think the decision through,
> you have to automatically feel that this is wrong, incorrect or
> unfair.

Some of these facets of a principled character are illustrated
through the story of Tata Finance. This was one of the most

unfortunate episodes in the history of the Tatas. Dishonesty by one or more individuals, compounded by poor corporate governance, led to significant financial losses and incalculable harm to the company. This should never have been permitted to happen. But the Tata Group responded in an exemplary manner. It admitted the lapse and did not brush it under the carpet. It also ensured that no depositor lost his money, going beyond strictly legal boundaries and honouring the trust that was at the heart of this contract.

A story of principle that is not told in this book is the narrative of why the Tata Group abandoned its bid for an airline. M.K. Kaw, the erstwhile civil aviation secretary in the Government of India, has briefly covered this in his book *An Outsider Everywhere: Revelations by an Insider*. He narrates an incident where Ratan Tata inquired about the chances of the minister clearing the Tata file. The Tatas, in partnership with Singapore Airlines, had submitted a proposal to start an airline. This could have changed the civil aviation landscape in the country. However, the approval from the minister never came; eventually the Tatas got tired of waiting and withdrew. It is reported that the Tatas had allegedly been approached to pay a bribe to expedite matters but this approach was promptly turned down.

The greater challenge with a principled approach is ensuring that it is ingrained in the organization. The Tatas have a comprehensive written code of conduct, by which all employees and partners are required to abide. Systems and processes of good corporate governance have been explicitly spelt out. However, as the British writer John Ruskin famously noted, 'honesty can never be based on policy'. Principles have to be embedded in an organization through tradition, values, walking the talk and a firm adherence to the code.

By and large, this has been the larger pursuit in Tata companies. However, as the number of businesses and employees grows, compromise of the P of Principle will perhaps be the greatest threat to the Tata Way. The words of Dr J.J. Irani, one of the most revered faces in the Tata Group, and a former director of Tata Sons, capture this threat quite well: 'You can never guard against a dishonest person. I believe it is human nature, and some people are basically honest and some people are basically dishonest; and the rest, a very large number, sit on the fence.'

The Tata Group is *not* a PERFECT organization

Many Indians expect the Tata Group to be a perfect organization just like they expect Mahatma Gandhi to be blemish-free. This isn't a reasonable expectation. We tend to put our heroes on pedestals, whether they are leaders, sportspeople or corporations. Then we expect, even demand, flawlessness from them because they are now on that pedestal.

The reality is that the Tata Group makes errors. It is fallible. It sometimes loses its way.

These lapses are not to be condoned, not at all. On the other hand, they should certainly lead to introspection as well as correction. This, I feel, is something that should be expected of any human endeavour. The aura of universal respect and infallibility that surrounds the Tata brand should not take away from this fundamental truth.

The Tata Way has to therefore necessarily deal with and learn from imperfection, while protecting and even enhancing the elements which create the pioneering, purposive and principled impulses.

Some stories in this book explore this area.

While the Tata Group responded in a credible manner to the

situation that arose in Tata Finance, there were lapses in corporate governance and a clear inadequacy of checks and balances, which could have detected evidence of dishonesty much earlier. There are valuable lessons here, which have been well digested.

The creation of the world's fourth fastest supercomputer by a Tata company was both a pioneering and a purposive venture, one that had been imagined for the first time ever by a private corporation. However, as you read this tale, you will see that there appears to be a slackening of purpose, and there is no clarity yet about the endgame. Will the Tatas or India make the world's fastest supercomputer in the years ahead? Only time will tell.

In the story of Tata Indica, there were early errors of product quality that were nearly fatal to the project. The company responded very quickly and comprehensively, and the car became a bestseller. However, something did go badly wrong, and had to be set right. Similarly, in the story of Tanishq and the jewellery business, there were once again early but extended errors in reading the consumer and the market, which led to prolonged losses. When these were corrected, the business made rapid progress.

Few corporates admit to being less than perfect unless they are compelled to, since this bruises the corporate ego. The Tata Group, on the other hand, has been more candid.

J.R.D. Tata, in his foreword to *The Creation of Wealth*, makes explicit reference to the Tata Group's 'remarkably consistent propensity, perhaps unavoidable in any pioneering and risky venture, for getting into difficulties in the early years of new projects, ultimately retrieving them by enormous and prolonged effort backed by a dour determination not to admit failure'.

Ratan Tata has publicly admitted that the Tata Nano, despite being a breakthrough innovation, was a wasted early opportunity. 'I don't think we were adequately ready with an advertising campaign, a dealer network,' he said. Few chairmen would say that. He also added that we would see a resurrection of this excellent product, as we move forward. In the past year, this has happened to a certain degree, and the Nano may yet become the fastest-selling car on the planet.

Pioneering, Purposive, Principled and not Perfect

As you read the log that follows, let these five words float in your mind. You will find their imprint in each story, in varying degrees. Perhaps they will, together with these tales and the *log* (people) in them, provide you a glimpse of the Tata Way.

Tata Indica, the Very First Indian Car

'Fortune favours the brave.'

—Virgil, *Aeneid*

'History may say that it failed. Or history may even say that it succeeded. All we know is that we thought of it, and we did it— we produced India's first car.'

—Ratan Tata, chairman, Tata Sons Ltd
and Tata Motors Ltd

The unveiling

Today cars have become items of intense desire. Consequently, auto shows have begun to rival fashion shows as far as the glamour quotient is concerned. Auto Expo 1998, held in New Delhi, was extra special because Tata Motors was launching an Indian car for the first time in history. Hundreds of children happily waving the Indian flag made the occasion festive rather than businesslike. To drive home the point further, the pretty car girls at the Tata pavilion were dressed in Indian attire, unlike the other pavilions where Western skirts were the norm. Cleverly gauging the mood that this car would be the showstopper at the Auto Expo, the organizers dressed up in smart sherwanis as well. And there, under the spotlight in the centre, stood the Tata car.

The Auto Expo is a biennial event that is held in the vast Pragati Maidan grounds. *Pragati* means 'progress' in Hindi— the arrival of the Tata car in January 1998 ensured that the grounds lived true to its name. An indigenously built Indian car was not merely a symbol of progress but an act of faith: few people had ever imagined that India would make its own car. The minister of commerce and industry, the late Murasoli Maran, saw the car at the expo and immediately called it 'The Kohinoor of India'. Like the legendary Kohinoor diamond, the car sparkled, attracting huge crowds.

The car itself had not yet been christened, but seeing the five prototype vehicles on display, the guest columnist for Rediff.com, Veeresh Malik, wrote about the car: '"like Zen" would be the best description, except for the fact that, unlike Zen, it has an excellently roomy rear seat. Test drives, however, were out for the moment. For those of you wondering, yes, it is likely that Telco [as Tata Motors was known then] will make, and sell, a world class car. It appears to be, frankly, like a cross between the Maruti Zen/Alto and the Mercedes Benz A-Class small car with cheaper specs.'

Vikram Sinha, who now heads the car manufacturing plant at Tata Motors, recalls being present at the unveiling. 'There was exceptional euphoria all over,' he says, and his eyes light up even today. 'There were endless queues to see India's first car, and I even met people who had come all the way from Mumbai just to take a look. What struck all of us was the feeling of patriotism and pride which flowed through that hall!'

Girish Wagh, who is now in the senior management team at

Tata Motors, and who has played a key role in spearheading development of the latest small car, Nano, was a young engineer in Tata Motors at that time. He recalls with pride that his father, who was a member of the Indica project team, was there at the auto show launch. 'My father called it one of the most fulfilling and satisfying days of his life,' he says, 'and that means everything to me.'

Patriotism, pride and courage

Cars have always been symbols of patriotism and pride. Famous auto brands such as Toyota, Rolls Royce, Mercedes Benz, Ford, Fiat and others have virtually been flag bearers for their respective countries. Yet, in the early 1990s, India, despite having launched missiles and spacecraft, did not have a car it could call its own, a car that had been designed and produced within the country. In 1993, Ratan Tata, chairman of Tata Motors, addressed the Automotive Component Manufacturers' Association of India in New Delhi, and suggested the possibility of component and car manufacturers in India getting together to produce an 'Asian car'. His intent was to emulate the Japanese and deliver a project worthy of national pride.

It was a good time to launch a brave new effort, because the Indian government—headed by P.V. Narasimha Rao, along with able economist Manmohan Singh as finance minister—had announced a slew of liberalization measures just a couple of years earlier, designed to take the country into a fast-paced growth trajectory, and eventually into the league of First World nations. History has shown that cars are often an engine of rapid economic growth all over the world.

Speaking on the reaction to this address, Ratan Tata said, several years later:

Needless to say, there was considerable criticism and cynicism about my suggestion. In the absence of a positive reaction, I decided that if we were not going to do this as a collaborative national effort, Tata Motors would undertake the lead effort. In 1995, we formally undertook a programme to develop a new Indian car. Two types of reactions were forthcoming at that stage: one was that we were being very brave but, the other, which came more often, was that we were being very foolish.

Both of these extreme reactions stemmed from two facts. First, Tata Motors had achieved fame and success as a maker of trucks and commercial vehicles—it had never made cars. Second, the venture was very expensive, entailing investments of around Rs 1700 crore, and could make or break the company's fortunes. Of course, this was not the first time that the chairman of the Tata Group was being faced with intense cynicism regarding a pioneering new venture, or being labelled 'foolish' for pursuing a courageous dream.

In a classic example of history repeating itself, here is a relatively ancient anecdote that took place more than ninety years ago, as told in *The Creation of Wealth*. This was when Jamsetji Tata, then chairman of the Tata Group, was pursuing steel manufacturing for the first time. Till 1903, India had never made its own steel. Lala recounts: '[When he heard about the Tata Steel venture] the Chief Commissioner for the Indian Railways, Sir Frederick Upcott, said—Do you mean to say that the Tatas propose to make steel rails to British specifications? Why, I will undertake to eat every pound of steel rail they succeed in making.'

A few years later, when the Tata Group had made a big success of the steel venture, Mr Dorab Tata, who succeeded Jamsetji as chairman, commented dryly, 'If Sir Frederick had carried out his undertaking, he would have had some slight indigestion.'

This time, while there was once again no dearth of naysayers who refused to believe in an Indian car, there are no reports of any of them offering to eat the car. Since the Indica weighs 995 kg and contains over 2000 steel components, it may have caused severe indigestion. On the other hand, many sceptics would have fit into this car with ease, because Ratan Tata was clear that the new car had to provide ample space for the typical Indian family. In his own words:

> We started out to design an Indian car from scratch. We felt that the Ambassador, much as it is maligned, is the ideal size for the travelling Indian public. So we decided to design a car with the internal volume of an Ambassador, the size of a Maruti Zen, and ease of entering and exiting, particularly for the rear seats. We thought of pricing it close to the Maruti 800, which is a very successful car, and adding the economy of diesel. Finally, we packaged this into a contemporary design.

These famous words became a clarion call to everyone in Tata Motors, as the company commenced the exciting and arduous journey of building India's first indigenous car, rising to the chairman's challenge.

Futuristic design

The first task was to finalize a design concept for the car, because most other things flow from the basic design. Ratan Tata led this path-breaking effort from the front. In this effort, he was perhaps also propelled by his own deep and abiding love for aesthetics and design.

The only cars that were seen in India those days were the Ambassador, the Premier Padmini and the Maruti 800. The original concepts for these cars had been created several years ago in countries outside India. None of these vehicles could be described as having exciting, contemporary designs. The first two vehicles looked and felt prehistoric when compared with the sleek modern cars one saw in Hollywood movies, but these dinosaurs stubbornly refused to go into extinction. Occasionally, a few beautiful but expensive imported cars also made it to Indian roads, and received envious glances from people who could never even think of owning or travelling in one of them.

If the Indica had to be world class, its design had to be comparable with the best in Europe and America. It had to be contemporary, appealing and so distinctive that it would sweep Indians off their feet. This task was assigned to the company's designers at the Engineering Research Centre located in Pune, commonly called the ERC. The designs were then refined and finalized in association with the famous Turin-based design house, I.DE.A. The ERC is a formidable facility, with a brilliant team of engineers. The designing process was completely automated at the centre using computer-aided design (CAD) and computer-aided manufacturing (CAM) stations, a novelty in those years. Tata Motors invested a massive sum of over Rs 120 crore on 225 CAD stations for its 340 engineers to work on.

When I visited the ERC during the writing of this book, it was buzzing with activity, as it must also have been during those early days of the Indica development, beginning in 1995. Several smart, young design engineers in the company got the rare opportunity to work on India's first car project. One of them was Ravindra Rajhans, a member of the core development team. Rajhans had graduated with a master's degree in industrial design from one of India's most-reputed engineering colleges, the Indian Institute of Technology (IIT), Mumbai. He had earlier worked on the styling of a light commercial vehicle (LCV) called the Tata 709, and also on the Tata Safari, a sports utility vehicle (SUV) that appeared to be a crossover between an LCV and a car. When he was asked to join the Indica team, he says he nearly fell off his chair.

> Those were heady days. We had the privilege of presenting our sketches and designs directly to our chairman, Ratan Tata. We were told that the design of the car would be developed by us, and finalized in collaboration with I.DE.A., a design house in Turin, Italy.
>
> I remember a meeting in Pune during September 1995, where some of us asked the chairman—'Sir, why are we going to Italy? Can't we do the design here, entirely in our own facilities in Pune?'
>
> His answer told us what the quest for world class meant. Mr Tata looked us in the eye, and said—'I believe totally in our own capabilities. But when we visit motor shows abroad, we see the great strides which global car companies have made, the excellent designs they have already launched in Europe and other Western countries. Our effort should be to leapfrog into the future. For this to happen we should work in the design environment of Europe, where the design ethos is well ahead of India. Then we can hope for a car which is ahead of its time.'

Turin was, therefore, a perfect choice; it is the design capital for the stylish Italian car industry, housing firms such as I.DE.A., and the headquarters of brands such as Fiat, Lancia and Alfa Romeo. It is also breathtakingly beautiful, surrounded on the western and northern fronts by the majestic snow-clad Alps. Natural beauty has always been a source of inspiration for intensely creative people such as designers.

Meanwhile, back home in Pune, a mammoth exercise in creativity and execution was under way: over 3800 components, 700-plus dies and 4000 fixtures for the Indica were being designed. These parts were also being simultaneously tested and validated, which was made possible by CAD systems that had been installed just in time for this project. In fact, paper drawings were done away with completely, which was an achievement in its own right.

Between Pune and Turin, the engineers at Tata Motors had to address several complicated design challenges. The car had to rise to Ratan Tata's challenge, and provide the space large enough for an Indian family. A typical Indian family has five or six people—husband and wife, two children and one or two grandparents who live in the same home. On long drives, the family also travels with a significant amount of luggage. One must not forget to mention here that this luggage will include tasty, freshly cooked home-made or local food. From personal experience, I can confidently say that this matter of food receives a lot of attention while planning a car journey.

For a product from the house of Tatas, which enjoys the trust of millions of Indians, safety had to be a zero-compromise feature. A colleague who lives in Europe, once commented on the car driving experience in India: 'How do you drive safely on roads where, on one side, autorickshaws are zipping by madly like Formula 1 cars, while on the other side cows are ambling as if the roads were their favourite meadows?'

The engine, which is at the heart of the car, had to provide excellent performance and mileage. Here, the Tata Motors team worked with Le Moteur Moderne (LMM), France, for engine testing and evaluation. The transmission system was designed entirely in-house, adding new capabilities to a company that had no background in cars. Accelerated learning became the mantra of the hour in all areas, simply because there was no in-house expertise of manufacturing cars to fall back on.

When the first prototype of the Indica was unveiled several months later, in some secrecy within Tata Motors, it was clear that this design effort had succeeded brilliantly. Everyone agreed that here was a car clearly ahead of its time; it looked very distinctive compared to other Indian cars of that period, and had an unmistakable international appeal. Everyone agreed that the car offered incredible space when compared to any vehicle of similar class. And the Indica met global crash test standards with ease. But at its heart it was an Indian car.

Rajhans recounts an interesting 'Indianness' story from his days in Turin.

> I remember the day the first design prototype of the Indica was finally ready, and it looked so beautiful. My colleague and I, who were deeply involved in the design effort, wanted to celebrate the occasion before shipping the prototype car to India. In Italy, they celebrate with champagne. But we were so proud of the Indianness of the car that we wanted to celebrate with a puja (prayer) to God Almighty, for having guided us in making our design so successful, so wonderful. To perform this traditional puja ceremony, we needed a coconut, *haldi* (turmeric) and *kumkum* (vermilion). But where do you find these in a place like Turin? We roamed virtually every road and cobbled street of Turin for an entire day, hunting for these three essential items. It was difficult, but we eventually found them. We conducted our Indian puja and left the broken coconut in the car, as a symbol of the Almighty's blessings.
>
> I am told that our colleagues back in India were most surprised to find the coconut, when they opened the shipment and unveiled the car!

Everyone who saw the prototype car remembers their first reaction even today.

Girish Wagh says that he first saw the purplish-blue Indica when he strolled into the prototype shop on some other work. 'Wow, what a wonderful new Toyota car!' was his first thought. It was only when he got closer that he realized it was not another vehicle from the Japanese Zen master of cars, but the new Tata car.

Some other reactions from the Tata Motors shop floor were equally euphoric. 'The first sight of the car was a "wow" moment for us. This was breakthrough styling, and we knew it as soon as we saw it!'

'The final design was chosen by Mr Tata, out of a few shortlisted concepts. We fell in love with it; we knew instinctively that we were backing a winning horse.'

Components of a world-class car

Even as the design concept was constantly being refined in collaboration with I.DE.A, work had also commenced on another big area—manufacturing or sourcing of components and vendor development.

The 3885 discrete designed components of the car now had to be locally developed and manufactured, either by Tata Motors or by capable vendors. Quick decisions were taken on which parts would be made internally and which outsourced. Either way, most of these were being made for the first time ever within the country. Global car companies such as Ford Motors and General Motors have grown on the back of strong vendor partners such as Visteon and Delphi, built over several decades. Tata Motors, on the other hand, did not have a vendor base for car parts. It had to develop this vendor community from scratch. It had to ensure that vendors met the global quality standards required, making it a task of herculean proportions.

One man who recalls this vividly is Dilip Huddar, who is now the general manager of strategic sourcing for the company. He was a key member of the Indica ancillary development team.

> Our mandate was to develop the supplier base for the new car. A special team was created, called SQIG—the Supplier Quality Improvement Group. We were told that over 500 cars would be made per day.
>
> Until then, our plant was manufacturing around 100 trucks or Sumo vehicles per day, so this was a huge mindset shift! We used to begin work at 6.30 a.m. to make this possible, and end the day pleasantly exhausted but never before midnight. There was so much to do and so little time. This was such a large and prestigious investment for us; we were determined to make it happen really well.

Another member of this team was Atul Chandrakant Bhate, who heads product development for the cars business today. He had joined Tata Motors in 1992, fresh from graduate school where he had studied mechanical engineering.

'I was terribly excited when I was selected for the cars project. On the very first day, we were told that we would be given intensive training by an expert named A.J. Agnew, on development of parts for cars. The message was very clear— this is a different ball game from trucks and commercial vehicles.'

A.J. Agnew had been worldwide director of supplier quality at the Cummins Engineering Corporation in the USA. It was clear that the Tata Group was sparing no effort to ensure a world-class car. Agnew made it clear that everything had to be aligned perfectly with the final quality of the car, which is what mattered to people buying the vehicle. He emphasized that even the smallest compromises were not to be accepted, that tolerances had to be very strict and narrow. A detailed thirteen-step quality improvement programme was immediately put in place.

Dilip Huddar recalls: 'Our vendors were initially shocked that they had to carry out so many big quality improvements. Some of them began asking, why invest so much money into improving quality when Indian consumers will be happy with less? We had to convince them that Indian consumers deserved more, and Indica was determined to provide them the best.'

Nonetheless, several entrepreneurs were very keen to supply parts to the first Indian car. This was a matter of real pride for them. Some of them had even unofficially seen drawings of the new car, which had fuelled their interest further. They were now insistent that they would supply, and they did. In the midst of such exciting work with individual vendors, yet another major development was pioneered by the company, which would soon become instrumental to the future of the Indian car industry. Tata Motors decided to float a holding company for manufacturing car components, called Tata AutoComp Systems Limited. This company then formed joint ventures with global giants for specific components, thus bringing the best possible expertise into the country from different parts of the globe.

A joint venture with Johnson Controls of the United States was established to produce car seats. A partnership with Ficosa of Spain produced rear-view mirrors. Radiators were produced by a third company that was formed in collaboration with Toyo, Japan. These are some of the countless partnerships that Tata Motors formed with various global players. These joint venture companies, under the umbrella of Tata AutoComp

Systems, today supply to a range of Indian and global vehicle brands, including Tata Motors, Ashok Leyland, BMW, Mercedes-Benz, Ford, Mahindra & Mahindra and Honda. Indica had not merely given India its first indigenous car; it also helped establish in the country a global supply chain for cars!

Apart from Tata AutoComp Systems, more than 300 vendors were developed, which supplied over 1000 high-quality parts. In turn, this created a stream of 12,000 jobs. Nearly 98 per cent of all parts used in the Indica were made in India, an amazing statistic for a country that had never before made its own car.

'We created the entire sheet metal vendor fraternity around Pune,' says Atul Bhate. 'Sheet metal used in cars is large and voluminous, so vendors had to be close to our car manufacturing plant.'

He goes on to add:

> Many vendors have also gained handsomely from the Indica car project. Several thousand jobs have been created at their units, and small fledgling factories have now become large, profitable enterprises with revenues running into hundreds of crore of rupees. They are today large, sophisticated units catering to an array of brands. Some of them are listed on the stock exchange, and even have styling studios of their own!

Where should the Indica be manufactured?

While components were being developed, thought was also being given to where the Indica would eventually be manufactured, bringing together thousands of these components and shaping them into a complete car.

As the story goes, the team at Tata Motors Pune had initially concluded that Indica cars should be manufactured inside a building called the E-block. This is a set of buildings located within the existing commercial vehicles factory of the company, where trucks and LCVs had been manufactured for several years. The managers who came to this conclusion were also ready with all supporting details and charts, and felt their decision was the most efficient approach. Then, Ratan Tata visited the plant and discussed the subject. He is reported to have asked for a pair of binoculars, which were duly given to him. Clutching these binoculars, he walked up to the terrace of this block and surveyed the surrounding areas. Standing there, he saw the barren land, over six acres large, adjoining the existing factory.

'That is where our cars will be manufactured,' he said, pointing to this vast tract of land. The need for a large, independent manufacturing unit for cars was proven right by several events that followed: the huge launch orders received for the Indica, the manufacture of other new cars such as the Indigo and Vista that were launched by the company in the following years and, of course, the rapid growth of the Indian car market.

'We thought of a unit for making Indica cars. He visualized a large, full-fledged car business that would transform the company. That was the difference,' says a senior manager, recalling this incident.

The car manufacturing facility

But what about the car manufacturing facility itself? A new manufacturing unit can cost around US$2 billion, or even more—a huge amount that could have broken the company's back or even rendered the project a non-starter. Here, again, Ratan Tata and his core team at Tata Motors took a road less travelled, and it made all the difference.

Here is Ratan Tata's description of how it all transpired:

Very often, in developing a car abroad, the cost of development is about US$800 million [approximately Rs 3400 crore] and the cost of manufacturing facilities is around US$2 billion [approximately Rs 8500 crore]. In comparison, the Indica project cost us US$400 million.

Looking for an inexpensive manufacturing facility, we found a disused Nissan Plant in Australia. It was run for fifteen minutes every day only to keep the hydraulics and pneumatics in working order. It was offered for sale and we paid about Rs 100 crore for it—barely one-fifth to one-sixth of what we would have had to pay for a new plant. Our engineers dismantled the plant, all 14,800 tonnes of machinery, and shipped it to India in some 600-odd containers, facilitating the construction of the plant in Pune. This itself was a challenge, as it had never been done before. There were nagging doubts about whether we could dismantle an entire car plant and rebuild it. So, we tagged and identified the parts, then took them apart and rebuilt the plant as we went ahead. Of course, we added considerable new equipment to make the plant self-contained.

You would need over two lakh adult human beings to reach a weight of 14,800 tonnes! In addition to shipping this huge weight across two distant continents, every part had to be carefully taken apart, so that it could be put back together. This herculean task was accomplished within six months, and over just sixteen shipments. What could have been a nightmarish effort was made to look effortless because of the determination and rigorous effort of the entire team.

Robots and the Indica

Apart from the Nissan factory that was rebuilt in India, the manufacturing facilities for the Indica comprise five different areas: the engine shop, where engines for the car are made; the transmission shop, where the gearboxes and gear transmission systems are made; the press and welding shop, where some parts are pressed into shape and then welded together; the paint shop, where the parts are painted; and the final assembly shop, where the entire car is assembled.

These shop floors are a delight to visit because they are a picture of the latest technology at work. They are normally buzzing with a constant stream of systematic activity, with hundreds of parts being made, transported, stored and stitched together.

When I walked through these buildings, I was also struck by how large they were, stretching almost endlessly. The senior engineers nodded. 'Yes,' they said. 'The assembly shop alone is more than half a kilometre long. Walking was taking too much time. So we began using bicycles to move through the shop floors.' Thus was created the unusual sight of young men bicycling within shop floors where India's first car was being created. With such distances being covered every day on foot or bicycle, no wonder these engineers look so fit and healthy.

The welding shop is an impressive place that gives a view of the huge technology leap made by the Tata Group; it is a veritable 'hall of robots'. It resembles a scene from a science fiction movie or an Isaac Asimov novel, with giant robots effortlessly picking up large car parts such as doors or fenders, handing them over to other robots that weld the parts, and cars that are in various stages of completion moving along fully automated pathways. At some points, multiple robots work together on complex manufacturing operations. There are over 450 robots in this single hall, so you will find more than one whichever way you turn.

All across the hall, a million sparks fly as welding guns

completely operated by robots and computers carve out shapes on the cars. The reddish-coloured robots are many times the size of a human being; their ability to lift such large pieces of heavy metal with ease is an accurate demonstration of their incredible strength. A layman like me felt at ease only because, being a science fiction buff, I believe in the first law of robotics (from Isaac Asimov). Every robot is designed to obey this law, which specifies that 'A robot may not injure a human being, or through inaction let a human being come to harm'!

The head of this welding shop and supreme commander of this army of robots is Abhijit Ghaisas, a soft-spoken engineer who walks with a certain sure-footedness and acknowledges greetings from several workers on the way.

'Robots are used here for welding because of their accuracy and repeatability. And of course because of ergonomic considerations, due to which human operators should not undertake some of these manually taxing tasks. We have three robotic lines here. And this is the first significant robotic line installed in India.'

The Indica rolls out

The final stage of manufacture is the assembly and testing of the cars. Today, the plant has capacity to roll out 1000 shiny new Indicas per day, all ready to hit the road. But this was not the case when the voyage began.

Four shop floor operators who assembled the first Indica car found the going very challenging. Umesh Dhule, Sanjay Kurne, Kishore Jape and Uday Urankar were young lads in the Tata Motors factory back in 1998. Still on the right side of twenty, and hailing from the smaller towns of Maharashtra such as Kolhapur and Ahmednagar, they had just completed their apprenticeships. They had grown up in difficult economic circumstances, and spoke Hindi with the lilting Marathi accent that is common to this belt.

> It took us eight full days to assemble the first Indica car. We did not even know the names of the parts, so how could we locate them properly? It took so long that we thought to ourselves, how are we ever going to meet consumer demand? We had heard that more than one lakh people had paid a lot of money and booked the Indica, and were now eagerly waiting for their car. Would we disappoint them?
>
> We told our college friends back home that we were making India's first car. They laughed at us, and they said—'How can we ever make a new car in our country? Cars like this are only made in America and Europe, not in India.'

This was unfortunately the prevailing mindset about India's capabilities. However, it must be stated that this perception stood somewhat modified when the same college friends heard that the Tata Group was behind this venture.

Goaded by a sense of urgency and a desire to fulfil consumers' orders without delay, the rate of manufacture increased rapidly from one car per day to fifty to 100. Today, a new Indica car emerges from the factory every fifty-six seconds. From eight days to fifty-six seconds, now that's a remarkable journey! A few interesting stories from this journey provide some insight into the company and its people, and some reasons why India's first car was delivered so well.

Ratan Tata used to visit the Indica manufacturing facilities quite often. On one such early visit, he promptly noticed operators fixing the rear strut of the car manually. The operator would have to bend up and down 600 times to complete this operation on 300 cars each day. Ratan Tata called his managers immediately. 'How can we expect our men to do this throughout their lives? Surely it will damage their health. We must provide an automation solution, on priority.' The engineering department, amidst all its hectic schedules, rose to the occasion and developed a fixture to semi-automate the operation. This made life incredibly easier for the operators, who remember this fondly even today.

Two years later, the Indica was yet to deliver profits, and the company was staring at a massive loss because its commercial vehicles business was also facing a bad market. But, as the four operators recall, the company still gave them a very good wage increase that year. 'Frankly, we did not expect this. Neither were we in any position to demand such an increase in our salary, because we knew the poor financial situation. But the company was generous to us. That is why we love our company; that is why we give all our effort and energy to making these cars with all our heart.'

The operators also recall with pride that Ratan Tata has always been accessible to them, has routinely stopped by to exchange a few words whenever he visited, and has respected their ideas. In fact, many ideas from the shop floor were shared with the designers and accepted. Worker empowerment and involvement also led to a very good implementation of the production process, contributing to the final smooth rollout.

The identical sentiment is expressed several years later by a young graduate engineer, Neil Kamal Gupta, who supervises many of these operators in the Indica assembly plant today. 'Our senior management respects us; they take our ideas on board. P.M. Telang and Girish Wagh [who head the company and car business operations, respectively, in 2012] have full trust and faith in us, and that always makes me feel on top of the world! I want our latest Indicas to delight the customer completely, and I will do everything I can do to ensure that.'

With such splendid and committed effort, the first Indica

rolled out from this assembly plant in the year 1999, just thirty-one months after development had commenced. Many people still vividly remember that it was a green Indica, a colour that is no longer manufactured today. Green was undoubtedly the right colour, given that the car was ready within three years, and it was now going full speed ahead. Everyone also remembers that Ratan Tata drove the first car, which was adorned with bright flowers. Many important dignitaries and the media were present for the celebrations.

After all, this was no ordinary vehicle. The name 'Indica' said it all: in ancient days, this was the name used by the mighty Greeks when they referred to India. Megasthenes, the Greek general and historian, wrote fascinating things about India in his famous book *Indica*. Now Indica was also the name by which the entire world would know India's equally exciting first car.

Here is a wishful piece of fictional modern history. If the Greek emperor Alexander the Great were alive and had visited India in these modern times, he would certainly have wanted to disembark from his famous horse, Bucephalus, and take a test drive of the Indica. He knew a thoroughbred steed when he saw one.

More car per car

Tata Motors also focused a lot of attention on marketing the car to Indians in an unforgettable and compelling manner. Once again, this was a very different proposition from the company's existing business of selling trucks and commercial vehicles to fleet owners. To address the task, a separate strategic business unit and marketing organization was formed. It established new car dealerships and authorized service centres across the country.

Ratan Tata and his team thought that providing customers a new experience in car buying was an important part of giving them a new car. To establish these experiential standards, the company's own flagship dealership Concorde Motors was formed. Initially established as a joint venture with Jardine International Motors, it soon expanded to fourteen showrooms in key cities such as Bangalore, Mumbai and Delhi. It was kept lean but very responsive to consumer needs, offering virtually everything—sales, service and spares. Its objective was also to set the standards for dealerships across the country.

The big question now was: what should the central consumer proposition of Indica be? How should the car differentiate itself from other international brands? How best should this story be told to the common man, who had never before imagined an Indian car?

Rajiv Dube, the commercial head of this project, who later rose to become president of the passenger cars business of Tata Motors, embarked on this exciting journey with a newly created marketing team. An officer of the Tata Administrative Service, Rajiv had earlier worked in Ratan Tata's office, and therefore knew the chairman's mind well. He spearheaded his team to create one of the most memorable marketing campaigns ever in the history of the Indian cars industry.

Working closely with them in creating the winning advertisements for Indica was the reputed advertising agency Draft FCB+Ulka. Ambi Parameswaran, executive director and CEO of Draft FCB+Ulka, and also one of the country's foremost exponents in the discipline of marketing, recounts the story of how this was done:

> For us, Indica was not just a car. It was India's first ambition to take on the world. It was Tata Motors' passion on wheels. A

conscious decision was made right from day one, to assume a confident, aggressive approach, to instil a sense of pride in owning a world-class Indian car.

But first, we said, let us just show the car to consumers, and find out what they think, what they see as the most appealing features. So we parked the Indica at Worli (a prominent location in Mumbai), and we invited people to open the car and get in. There was tremendous response. Curiosity was so high; people just wanted to have a look at India's first car.

This was the same response that many managers of Tata Motors had experienced when they had taken the Indica for test drives on the roads of Pune. Ravindra Rajhans, the design engineer who had worked in Turin, narrates this story:

I was driving an Indica late at night, around 10.30 p.m., a few months before it was launched. It was dark, and suddenly I saw a motorcyclist chasing my car. I was very apprehensive, having heard a few terrifying stories about highway robberies and dacoities. I drove faster, but so did the motorcyclist behind me. Eventually he overtook me, parked in front of my car, and stopped me from going further. I was now seriously worried, and prepared for the worst.

The motorcyclist got down, along with a small boy who was on the pillion behind him. He said that his son wanted to see India's car—that was why he had been chasing me for so long. They saw the car and spent a few minutes appreciating it from all over. Then they thanked me and went away!

Apart from sheer curiosity, what did the hundreds of people who got into the Indica at Worli have to say? Listen to Parameswaran once again:

People were pleasantly surprised that the Tata Group had made such a good-looking car. They asked us time and again, in Hindi—'*Yeh gaadi Tata banata hai? Yeh toh badi garv ki baat hai.* (Does the Tata Group make this car? This is truly a matter of pride.)'

Everyone who opened the car was also delighted with the amount of space inside the vehicle. They kept saying there was far more space than they ever imagined.

These two insights—the hyper-curiosity it generated and the feedback that this was a great-looking car with lots of space inside it—were used to create the first advertisement campaign for the Indica.

Before the launch, a teaser advertisement further stoked curiosity, as it announced: 'India's most eagerly awaited car'. It created huge anticipation and lots of conversation around it. This tagline became so famous that it was picked up by the media and used extensively, even in unrelated areas. When India had a new prime minister soon after the launch of the Indica, this development was announced in newspapers as 'India's most eagerly awaited prime minister'!

However, even more famous and impactful than this teaser tagline was the next advertisement in the launch campaign. Building on the fact that the Indica offered more good looks, more space and more engine power, this advertisement described the vehicle as 'More car per car'.

This line was the result of inspired creative thinking, motivated by what consumers had said and several rounds of internal discussion with the Tata Motors team. Earlier lines such as 'The complete car' and the 'No compromise car' were discarded in favour of a line that exhibited attitude and total confidence. This was a perfect example of a resurgent India taking on the world. 'More car per car' became a phrase on everyone's lips soon after these advertisements appeared in newspapers and on hoardings across the country. In the final analysis, the line 'More car per car' was perhaps so successful because it was a perfect summation of Ratan Tata's clarion call, which had driven the entire Indica project from start to finish: 'A car with the internal volume of an Ambassador, the size of a Maruti Zen, the economy of diesel and pricing close to the Maruti 800.'

The Indica received a fabulous response, the best ever in India's history till the time. The car garnered 1,15,000 'fully paid' bookings within eight days of its launch. This was many multiples more than the bookings obtained by other international cars launched during the same period. This also showed the tremendous enthusiasm with which Indians had welcomed the first car they could call their very own. Within a few months, the Indica had notched up a commendable market share of more than 14 per cent in its segment.

The unbeatable pull of the Indica was acknowledged by the competition in many other ways. Just a few hours before the Indica was formally launched by Tata Motors at the vast Turf Club grounds in Mahalaxmi, Mumbai, the market leader Maruti Suzuki announced a significant drop of Rs 25,000 in the price of its flagship car, the Maruti 800. This was perhaps on Ratan Tata's mind when he went on stage that evening to present the Indica to the crème de la-crème of the city. 'Thanks to Tata Motors,' he said, 'whichever car you choose to buy, you will now get more.'

The Agony and the Ecstasy

Many decades ago, the author Irving Stone titled his famous biography of Michaelangelo *The Agony and the Ecstasy*, in an attempt to capture the extreme emotional states that this genius experienced throughout his life. The same title best describes the first three years of the life of the Indica. Initially, there were several accolades, including record bookings that resulted in strong market shares. But dark clouds quickly gathered on this sunny horizon, and the company had to suddenly deal with a wave of unanticipated consumer complaints. Essentially, these revolved around several product quality issues that cropped up immediately after the launch.

Several consumers called in, complaining of high noise and vibration levels in the car. There were problems relating to winding the windows up and down. Performance of the engine came in for criticism. Word of mouth was quickly turning from highly positive to highly negative. Some Tata Motors veterans recall that this was not just a few isolated cases, but a flood of angry complaints. They wince, even today, when they speak about how customers turned violent at several locations. On the back of such negative feedback, sales of the Indica plummeted during the year 2000–01. Tata Motors announced its largest ever loss of Rs 500 crore during that year, and a few experts promptly blamed this loss on the failure of the Indica, and the company's decision to enter the passenger cars market.

The competition became hyperactive and began to write premature epitaphs for the Indica. A constant refrain heard in those days was that Tata Motors and Ratan Tata had made a big mistake in betting on an indigenously made car. And there is of course no dearth of condescending Western and Indian minds who never miss an opportunity to take potshots at India and other developing nations, which remain, in their minds, lands that are best suited to snake charmers, forests and elephants.

So was this the sad end of the Tata dream to make India's first car? Would it spell disaster for Tata Motors, which had made the back-breaking investment of Rs 1700 crore in the Indica project? Like the *Titanic*, had the Indica hit a fatal iceberg? Would it now drag down with it one of the most venerable companies of the Tata Group?

These were the heavy thoughts playing on everyone's mind when Ratan Tata called an emergency internal meeting at the Taj President Hotel in Mumbai, to take stock of the unfortunate situation and chart the way forward. Memories of that session are still vivid in the minds of many. Senior team members were encouraged by the chairman to vent their feelings of what had gone wrong, for as long as they wished. Many of them were sharply self-critical. It was clear that the huge financial loss had touched their souls, and the mounting customer complaints had hurt their pride. But, deep within, there was great resilience, undying hope, a commitment to make the venture a success.

Ratan Tata then steered the meeting in the direction of the improvements that were required. The conversation quickly converged on to what the team should address immediately. There was acknowledgement that some specific design flaws had to be rectified, even if this meant alterations in the basic design.

In the meanwhile, 'retrofit camps' were organized, where over 45,000 Indica cars were repaired, with forty-two parts being replaced entirely at the company's cost. Customer meets were held in every nook and cranny of the country, with a patient ear being given to every angry customer, and solutions being offered wherever possible. Senior managers from the marketing, design and manufacturing teams participated in these meets.

The Tata Motors team knew that pride and survival were simultaneously at stake. Of course the company had stumbled, and had to pull itself up very quickly. The chairman was leading this effort from the front, and all product changes necessary had to be implemented on a war-footing. There was some writing on the wall already, and there was little time left to erase it.

If courage is required to launch a breakthrough exploration to unknown lands, guts of steel are required to sustain the voyage when it runs into such rough seas. The team at Tata Motors proved itself equal to this daunting task. Working with Formula 1-like speed, they developed and implemented the required design changes. Vendors produced these altered parts. A new, robust Indica was ready by 2001, with key quality problems having been completely eliminated. It was launched in the market as Indica V2.

The word 'V2' announced the change loud and clear. This was also a technical-sounding suffix, therefore appropriate for a car. If Indica had been 'More car per car', the new Indica V2 was 'Even more car per car'. A fantastic television advertisement, which highlighted the product features of the new car, even as it re-emphasized the many positives of the original Indica, also helped build consumer conviction.

An interesting sidebar is worth mentioning here. This advertisement ended with a scene of several oriental-looking people, including the Indian actor Kelly Dorjee, bowing to the new Indica V2, in a tribute to its features. The thought was perhaps to depict the Indica V2 as being so good that even the Japanese, who are the masters of car making, pay salute to it. Such exaggeration is of course the lifeblood of good advertising. However, the Korean car company Hyundai used this scene as a basis to launch a complaint against this ad film with the Advertising Standards' Association of India (ASCI). While this complaint was eventually not upheld, it highlights the impact the new Indica V2 and its advertisement campaign had on its competitors.

Indeed, the impact of the Indica V2 was extraordinary and immediate. It marked not merely the revival of the Indica but its brilliant success. It became the fastest-selling automobile in Indian history when it completed sales of 100,000 cars in less than eighteen months. Despite an overall economic slowdown in 2001, it recorded a growth of over 46 per cent in that year, whereas most international competitor brands clocked only single-digit growth during the same period. The market share zoomed to over 20 per cent during the year 2001–02.

The commercial success was accompanied by other accolades too. Ratings of the Indica V2 by the J.D. Power study, a fiercely independent and widely respected review of cars, jumped dramatically. The 2003 J.D. Power India customer satisfaction study ranked the Indica diesel car as the best in the operating costs category, even ahead of the market leader, Maruti 800. The reputed television programme *BBC Wheels* declared the Indica the 'best car in the Rs 3 lakh to Rs 5 lakh price category'.

The confidence was back there were big smiles all around. There had been a rather large hiccup, but the team at Tata Motors had proven itself more than equal to it. India's first indigenously designed car had conclusively proven that it was an indisputable success.

More than the Indica

The Indica transformed Tata Motors from a successful truck maker to a modern automobile company, very sensitive to the pulse of consumers. A series of successful cars and SUVs have been launched by the company in the wake of the Indica, including the Indigo, the Vista, the Manza and the Aria. And, of course, the Nano, which has received universal acclaim as one of the most significant innovations in cars after the Ford Model T. Today, Tata Motors consistently occupies either the second or the third rank in the large Indian cars market, and the day is not far when (and here we borrow a phrase from Turin) it will aim to be Numero Uno.

The Indica also served as the perfect catalyst for transforming the car industry in India, ushering in the modern era, in the wake of economic liberalization in the country. It established the supply chain for the indigenous manufacture of cars by developing a range of competent vendors and collaborating with the best names in the world. This has served as a natural platform for many other global brands of cars to make their entry into India. It re-established Indian pride in engineering and manufacturing. By making India one of the few countries in the world to produce its own indigenously designed car, it emphasized that the engineering sector in the country was alive, vibrant and kicking.

It became a symbol of Indian prowess in developing world-class consumer products. The Indica was yet another pioneering venture by the Tata Group, going where no Indian company had gone before.

The heart of courage

I often wonder: where does such great courage come from? Does it come from deep within outstanding individuals and teams, as they pursue their passions and dreams? Does it emerge from a very strong sense of duty to the country, to society or, in a more limited sense, even to one's family? Or does it simply come from fearlessness, which often lends itself generously to a noble purpose?

Here is what Ratan Tata has to say about the Indica, the spirit and the heart of courage. 'I think we were more brave than foolish actually. Over the years, TELCO had introduced a series of products that took to the Indian roads, competed with Japanese products when those were introduced, and found their rightful place in the country.' He was referring here to commercial vehicles made by the company, such as the successful 407 and 709 series, as well as crossover vehicles such as the Tata Estate, Sierra, Sumo and Safari.

'In addition, I had faith in TELCO's engineers.' His belief in the company's engineers, particularly the 300-odd young engineers who were raring to go, was an important starting point for embarking on the voyage of the Indica.

'Can we do something that has never been done before? I would like to believe that it can be done. We can make it happen; we just need to make sure that we do it.'

'It is important, particularly for the younger people in India, to believe in what we are doing and that we can do much more. I hope the younger generation will take India to new heights, which I am sure they can. They need to believe in and recognize the potential of their own capabilities.'

The road ahead

Fourteen years after the Indica was launched, there are still many big challenges ahead of the Tata Motors cars business. Competition from large international brands with deep pockets and global resources has only got tougher. Achieving larger scale is even more critical today to keep costs low. Consumers have become more demanding, and ensuring world-class quality of products and services is essential. However, for a company that successfully created India's first car, taking a path that was so different, refreshing and challenging, this will only create multiple springboards for many more acts of courage.

Uplifting Tales from Okhamandal

'In every community there is work to be done. In every nation, there are wounds to heal. In every heart, there is the power to do it.'

—Marianne Williamson, spiritual activist and author

'My view is that our expression of social responsibility cannot be measured in terms of profit or cost. It is our contribution to whichever nation our companies operate in, and an expression of goodwill to the communities around us. It cannot be quantified in the language of sales or turnover. I would like to think this is the best part of what Tata companies stand for.'

—Ratan Tata, chairman, Tata Sons

Beauty and irony in Okhamandal

Okhamandal lies at the tip of the Saurashtra peninsula in Gujarat, the westernmost state of India. Beauty and irony coexist here. It is home to Dwarka, where the beautiful temple of Lord Krishna attracts millions of pilgrims throughout the year. Pilgrims find both peace and joy in the image of the lord, the stone pillars and the intricately carved spire of this ancient temple, whose origins date back to 400 BCE. It is also the location of several serene and unspoilt beaches, lapped softly by the waters of the Arabian Sea. Sitting on one of these beaches late at night, my wife and I could feel the cool, salty breeze caress our cheeks as we gazed at the stars in the crystal clear dark skies.

This area is a mosaic of many diverse tribes and communities, some of them unique to the region—the tall strapping Vaghers and the nomadic Rabaris. It is also the abode of the Aahirs, Lohanas, Rajputs, Harijans, Brahmans and Muslims—the colourful, vibrant and hardy people of Okhamandal.

Yet the irony is that this land, which is surrounded by water on three sides, has lived with the misfortune of being an arid, drought-prone region. In the 1980s, four continuous years of drought wrought havoc on the community, leaving only the hardy thorn bushes standing, mute spectators to these acute hardships. Even drinking water was hard to come by. Underground water, in the few places where it was found, was brackish and undrinkable beyond the depth of thirty feet. The poet Samuel Taylor Coleridge could well have been thinking about Okhamandal when he wrote, 'Water, water every where / nor any drop to drink'.

The city of Mithapur in Okhamandal is also home to Tata Chemicals, one of the largest companies of the Tata Group. With businesses spanning chemicals, fertilizers, salt and other consumer products, the company has set itself a noble mission of 'serving society through science'. The company has a proud presence in four continents today: Asia, Africa, Europe and North America. But Mithapur, the city of salt, is where it all began.

Tata Chemicals first made its presence felt when the Maharaja of Baroda Sayajirao invited the Tata Group to assist in the making of a product of national importance—salt—over seventy-five years ago. In its long history, the company has innovated successfully to overcome several difficulties, including the lack of water. Today, its factories are vibrant, its vast salt pans hug the earth and Mithapur is one of the finest living spaces in the country. Here, a new factory has also just been erected, using the latest technology, to cater to the rapidly growing consumer demand for Tata Salt. I also discovered that a visit to the Mithapur factory is an excellent practical lesson in chemistry.

This is also where Tata Chemicals has been quietly transforming an entire community. Stretching well beyond Mithapur city, families in forty-two villages of Okhamandal have embraced exciting new possibilities that have lifted their lives. These are economically poor and educationally backward villages inhabited by several tribes, making the challenge doubly difficult. But there's been a catalyst: the Tata Chemicals Society for Rural Development (TCSRD), which has created a powerful programme. Its energetic activities have touched thousands of lives: first with adequate water, then ample affection and finally a little bit of magic.

Alka Talwar, the restless and energetic head of community development at Tata Chemicals, says:

> Corporates are often neighbours of necessity. We want to become a neighbour of choice. We love Okhamandal; this land is sacred; it is our home. We want to make this community blossom in every way we can, overcoming every challenge it faces. But we don't believe in charity or in a benevolent approach. We want to make this effort sustainable by teaching and empowering every segment of our community how to fish for themselves and become self-reliant.

The three short tales I am about to narrate here will illustrate how a company that genuinely cares can create a remarkable and sustainable new future for its community.

The dreamers of Tupni

In the small village of Tupni in Okhamandal the land is rocky and the groundwater resources are extremely limited. The clear blue sky over this village, with not a wisp of cloud in sight, contrasts with the dusty brown soil. The Ahirs, a robust Gujarati tribe with a strong build, heavy gait and deep voices, live here.

Many years ago there lived a young man called Pala Pitha. Just like all of us he dreamed of a prosperous future for his family. But he also knew that like most other dreams in Tupni his dreams were destined to die quickly, because the village was very dry. There was no water here for drinking or farming. His mother, Doshima, who had no money to buy oil for her home, was wise enough to understand that dreams alone cannot light her kitchen fires. So she carried with her bowls of bajra, the rough grain grown on her dry land, and bartered it for small bowls of oil. The arid earth only permitted bajra and jowar to take birth in its soil, and that too if the rain gods permitted. Pala Pitha's only source of income was the water that he delivered to the villagers at the measly rate of five rupees a barrel. Did he really have the right to dream?

The first signs of water appeared when the villagers constructed a check dam after raising funds within the community. People from the nearby Tata Chemicals factory were seen in the village for many months before this happened, and a big excavator from the company also appeared just before the construction commenced. The check dam was meant to capture rainwater during the monsoon and store it for use throughout the year. This ensured cultivation on farms for the greater part of the year. As more water became available, yields of groundnut jumped up from ten maunds (one maund is twenty kilos) a bigha (a measure of land equivalent to 0.4 acres) to eighteen maunds a bigha. The possibility of a second winter crop, such as of *jeera* (cumin), also opened up.

Over time, this dam also helped raise the water table in the surrounding area, but most importantly it raised the confidence of Tupni. From such confidence came many more wells that were dug by individuals, and from these wells came much more water. A village that had been damned by nature had been dammed by its own people.

A confident Pala Pitha now had more crops to sell because he had begun digging his own wells. When his income met his basic requirements comfortably, his dreams for prosperity came to fruition. Today, he owns two tractors, a house and a motorcycle. His wife doesn't have to roam the streets bartering bajra for oil, like his elderly mother once did. Both his children have been born into a more promising future. The memories of carrying barrels of water for others have receded into history.

Vajsibhai Lakhumanbhai Chavada, the head of watershed management of Tupni village, is dressed in flowing white clothes and seated on the spacious veranda of a colourful brick house with a large courtyard. As Vajsibhai speaks, the women of the house listen keenly to our conversation.

> Yes, those difficult times are in the very distant past, and we thank Tata and TCSRD for that. Your teams made these dreams possible for us. You know, when TCSRD first came to our village with talk of this watershed project, the first meeting was held right here. This was a very small mud hut at that time. We spoke about the immense benefit for our farms. We

asked for contributions of Rs 500 from each household to build the check dam. Our villagers asked: Will Tata Chemicals run away with our hard-earned money? How do we know our money will be safe? The meeting broke up with a lot of noise and no decision.

A few people later met me and said, governments have promised us similar things so many times, and this is the first time non-government people are coming here and insisting on our contribution. We though Tata is like a cat: they will come to our house and lap up the milk and cream and run away. So I told them, 'We need to believe in this; all my information says they are good people. In any case, cats are very useful because they catch mice!'

Guided by TCSRD, Vajsibhai and his core team hit upon the brainwave of conducting an entry-level activity to build confidence in the village that their money would be safe. They made a *chabootara* (a raised platform) for pigeons, worth Rs 5000, after collecting small amounts from the villagers. The chabootara came up very well, and people felt reassured that their money would be in good hands.

After that, it took Vajsibhai another six months to persuade the villagers to contribute to the building of the check dam. Finally, a gram sabha (village council) was held, where the credentials of Tata Chemicals were discussed threadbare, and eventually the proposal was approved for the first dam. Collecting money from the villagers was still a difficult proposition. Vajsibhai recalls that at the start of the collection drive, no villager appeared. It took three more months and countless meetings to collect Rs 25,000 and start the construction of the first dam. They called it Ravji.

The rest, as they say, is history. Plans were made; resources were mapped; a project schedule was worked out. TCSRD coordinated this entire process and provided technical help. However, the actual construction was done by the villagers themselves, piling on the excavated earth in tall mounds. Their ownership was very high and very consistent, particularly because their own money had been invested. Within three months, the check dam was ready!

As soon as work on the Ravji Dam started and people saw the progress, a second group came forward with an advance contribution for the next dam (Mataji Dam). After that there was no looking back and they collected Rs 1.45 lakh.

Vajsibhai and his younger colleague Mesurbhai conclude:

> Now we can think of the future. Because water is available, we have water taps at home. We have dreamt of tractors and motorcycles. We have dreamt of good brick houses. Some of us have dreamt of staying at one place, rather than leading the difficult life of being nomads chasing water. So, migrations have stopped. We have made all these dreams come true in the last few years. And now we are also dreaming of education for our children, for them to become engineers and doctors.

From sheer subsistence to dreaming of higher education, the small village Tupni in Okhamandal has come a long way. This was the first watershed project undertaken by TCSRD. The initiative later spread to twenty-seven villages and created prosperity in all of them. Over 2400 water harvesting structures have been constructed, including check dams, bunds, percolation tanks and farm ponds. The latest and most ambitious initiative, launched in 2012, is the six-kilometre-long Gomti Canal to carry water for irrigation, built with voluntary contributions from 120 farmers. Standing by the side of this impressive canal on a burning summer day, I spoke to a farmer. All he said was: 'This is my canal, this is my future.'

Villagers are involved at every step, and a system of Participatory Rural Appraisals put in place by TCSRD ensures that systematic mapping and feedback is completed before work begins. The water storage capacity in these villages has now exceeded 240 million cubic feet, and both the quantity and the quality of water have improved. Today, villagers happily contribute up to 40 per cent of the expenditure of constructing newer dams, and the government and TCSRD chip in with the balance.

The direct economic gains to villagers, arising from higher crops and yields, have been significant and run into several crore of rupees. However, the indirect gains have been equally impressive: creation of new assets, higher confidence, increased natural resource awareness, a sense of unity and, now, a desire for higher education for their children.

Alka Talwar says:

> At Tata Chemicals, we knew water well; we had a long relationship with water because our company had struggled with availability of fresh water required for manufacturing for a very long time. We took this knowledge to the community, and it worked. But the most important breakthrough, I think, was winning the confidence of the villagers and obtaining their own contributions. This instils local ownership, and makes the effort sustainable.

A final word about the dreamers of Tupni: when one dream is achieved, they begin chasing another. Vajsibhai and some other villagers led us into a small brick godown. As soon as we entered we were engulfed by an aroma. This was the winter's harvest of jeera grown on their farms. We bit into a few seeds— it was easily the most flavourful jeera I had ever tasted!

Vajsibhai turned to the TCSRD team, laughed and said,

'The water you brought us has created this. Now, tell me, how can Tata Chemicals also help us market this excellent crop of jeera to the world?'

The weavers of Okhai

In Okhamandal, not far from Tupni, lies the village of Arambdha, populated by the Rabari tribe, among others. Arambdha may soon rival Kancheepuram or Banaras, or even Milan, because of the promising young women there who want to create the world's finest handicrafts brand. In this astonishing story of community development, we'll see how a resolutely determined woman, Ramiben Nagesh, and her friends set up the Okhai brand and how Tata Chemicals helped them along the way.

Ramiben is a Rabari woman. Garbed in bright red tribal attire, she sports large gold earrings and heavy, long neckwear. The entire length of her hands is tattooed with a traditional pattern. She speaks with infectious enthusiasm about life in Arambdha.

The Rabari women are talented but have little formal education. The area they live in is dry and prone to severe water shortages. The community is economically backward and does not naturally encourage women to pursue careers of any kind, beyond taking care of the family's livestock.

Several years ago, Ramiben joined a woman's self-help group set up by TCSRD, designed to empower women and help them to generate income for themselves. In 2002, she heard about a very different and creative effort that was also being established by the same organization, to create and popularize handicrafts from the Okhamandal region, under a brand called Okhai (which means 'from Okhamandal').

Ramiben's curiosity was piqued because colour and artwork

are all-pervasive in Rabari homes. Colourful dhurries (called *godhda*s) are woven for use by family members and house guests. The walls of their huts are decorated with appliquéd and finely embroidered wall hangings. These walls are often repainted immediately after weddings, with images of men, women, animals and birds set in striking patterns. Many Rabari designs also incorporate interpretations of Lord Krishna, as represented at the Dwarka Temple. Like all the other children in a Rabari household, Ramiben was taught art from a very young age by the family elders.

Ramiben could feel the kindling of her creative urges when the handicraft development project began so she enlisted the support of her husband and mother-in-law and joined the team at Mithapur. In the early days she worked on pillows, bed sheets and wall decorations. It was fun being surrounded by colourful designs, and she was paid well for her efforts.

Then, one fine morning, Alkaben (as Alka Talwar is fondly referred to by these women) told her that she would have to travel to Ahmedabad to meet a fashion designer. Ramiben was perturbed because she had never left home to traverse such a distance. But the promise of breaking through a new knowledge barrier provided the necessary impetus to this courageous woman.

A few other Rabari women accompanied Ramiben on this life-changing visit. Ramiben's meeting with Rupali Agarwal, a reputed designer from Gujarat, was a meeting between raw talent and sophisticated design sensibility. Rupali walked all of them around the brightly lit showrooms of Ahmedabad, the cuts that appeal to modern women, the design processes involved and the need to simultaneously maintain originality. Ramiben returned, rejuvenated, to Mithapur, her head milling with a thousand different design ideas.

Ramiben and her colleagues incorporated many of Rupali Agarwal's inputs as they went about creating lovely kurtas, kurtis, bedcovers, tablecloths, shawls, skirts, aprons and bags. There are purple patterns on black, blue floral patches on orange, exquisite beadwork, bold embroidery and innovative mirrorwork. There is a special mural that depicts village scenes, authentic and modern at the same time, clearly made with great love and care. When my wife and I saw these products at the Okhai showroom in Mithapur, we fell instantly in love with them, and my wife ended up buying several pieces all at once. All of these products proudly carry the ethnic designs of Okhamandal that are now interpreted with increasing sophistication and finesse.

Ramiben says:

> Now we think of designs all the time. Recently, when a customer went into the trial room to test out a garment, we asked her permission, took her dress and traced out the design, so enamoured were we of that particular design. We live in a world of designs. We watch carefully the designs of newsreaders and television personalities. And we are constantly thinking, why can't we make cuts such as these, or even better ones, and marry them with our designs?

Ramiben and hundreds of other women have risen beyond their traditional confines as keepers of livestock, and have leveraged their rich Rabari traditions to achieve economic independence and build new careers for themselves.

The guardians of the Okhai brand come from varied backgrounds. Meet Lakuben, a Rabari woman and an expert master cutter of Okhai garments today. In her previous job she was as a manual labourer, cutting and crushing stones for a paltry sum of money. Khatijaben, a Muslim woman and one of the oldest members of Okhai, is in charge of quality control. She is the sole breadwinner in her family and pays for her daughter's education primarily with her earnings from Okhai. Further down in an adjacent building is Zareena Kureshi, a young bubbly girl and master cutter who declares, 'Okhai is my life.' She says the training that Okhai provided her at the National Institute of Fashion Technology, one of the finest institutes of the country, has opened her eyes to a fresh new world.

Okhai has an efficient production system in place: cut cloth is sent to women in their villages, along with a work kit, and collected once the work has been done. According to Alka Talwar, 'This allows them to work in their village environment, at a time of their choice.'

Three hundred women earn their livelihoods from Okhai today, and hundreds more will join in the years ahead. Earnings of around Rs 1000 a month are normal, and women can earn more or less based on the hours of work they invest. The women have used this money primarily to educate their children.

Ramiben says:

> Looking after goats and cows is fine upto a point, but we need a better future for our children. You need education to do well in today's world. So, I have told my husband, let's run the household with your earnings. And let's use my earnings from Okhai to give our children good schooling and high education.
>
> I appeared for my twelfth standard exams recently; my work at Okhai has given me the confidence to study even more. My children are very happy that their mother is also studying, and when I returned from the exam hall they asked me with a stern expression, 'Mummy, have you done well in your exams?'

Ramiben has gained enough confidence to host the International Women's Day celebrations at Mithapur. All the craftswomen I met spoke in a similar fashion, with passion and confidence.

Meanwhile, sales of Okhai have more than tripled in three years, from 7000 pieces in 2009 to 26,000 pieces in 2011. Today, Okhai has showrooms in Ahmedabad and Mumbai, and over fourteen other distributor outlets across India. Regular exhibitions are also held in several parts of the country. Seeing the immense potential, TCSRD has now created an independent organization called Okhai Centre for Empowerment. A business manager has been appointed to drive marketing initiatives and popularize the brand. The objective is to make Okhai a self-sustaining and profitable business, which will provide empowering opportunities to many more women.

Of course, the challenges of competing with well-heeled fashion and handicrafts brands are quite daunting. There is significant work to be done in areas such as the constant creation of new designs, brand building and developing convenient retail access across the country. Yet, Alka Talwar and her team are quietly confident, because their belief in their mission is unwavering. They look at me and they say, 'Creating the next Ramiben, the next Zareena, that is our constant goal. That is the core of Okhai. Certainly it is a big challenge, but when we think of the impact on these women and the community, we feel very happy and we smile.'

Vhali, the gentle whale shark

Vivek Talwar, who until a few years ago was the head of community development in Tata Chemicals, has an innate talent for storytelling.

Around the coastline of Okhamandal is a unique marine world. There are rich coral reefs, lush mangrove stands, turtle nesting beaches and bird roosting areas. For many months each year, these seas are also home to the whale shark, the largest fish on our planet. This is not a whale, but a docile fish that is as large as a whale. It can grow up to fourteen metres long, which is larger than the length of a bus! It comes to the seas off the Okhamandal coast to breed from March to May each year, and also as part of its natural migration pattern.

Unfortunately, during the 1990s, the coastal towns of Gujarat had also become the killing fields of the whale shark. Despite being an endangered species, whale sharks were slaughtered indiscriminately in towns such as Dwarka, Madhavpur, Mangrol, Veraval and Diu. Nearly 1000 were killed each year. In May 2001, the whale shark was officially declared an endangered species, which has significantly helped its protection status.

The meat and liver of the fish were sold, with each giant fish fetching as much as Rs 1 lakh, a bonanza for fishermen. Of course, this was also happening because fishermen were not aware that the whale shark was endangered, or that it was a species that required protection. In fact, whale sharks were referred to quite derogatorily as 'barrels', since they were hunted down with barrels.

Since the whale shark is an integral part of the rich biodiversity of this area and Tata Chemicals has historically played a role of community developer, we strongly felt the need to intervene and contribute whatever we could to save this species.

So we got moving, and we moved fast. To save the whale shark, we knew we had to increase awareness significantly among everyone in the region, most importantly among the fishermen. We had to build in the people of Okhamandal and Gujarat pride in the fact that this giant fish is a visitor to our seas, and change the mindset that saw it as an animal fit only for slaughter.

Tata Chemicals backed us completely, with all the resources that we needed. Prasad Menon, who was managing director at that time, had only one condition that he wanted us to fulfil. He wanted this to be a world-class conservation effort.

I also remember a brief meeting with Mr Ratan Tata, who displayed keen interest immediately, and strongly encouraged us to take forward the project. 'These are endangered creatures; we must do this,' he said. And then he also told us, as a personal aside, 'I have swum with the whale sharks. It was such a beautiful experience.'

Tata Chemicals partnered with the Wildlife Trust of India and the International Fund for Animal Welfare, who were at the forefront of this programme. Their experience in the area helped give direction to our ideas. To create maximum impact, we brought to this project the same high levels of innovation which we bring to our business.

To begin with, we needed a powerful new brand ambassador who would help us promote the whale shark. We even wondered if it would be wise to bring in a popular Bollywood actor like Shahrukh Khan, like so many brands do. After some discussion, we chose an unconventional but apt ambassador for the project: Morari Bapu, a highly revered religious leader of Gujarat. Fishermen and the general public would listen to him; his emotional connect and credibility were very high.

Morari Bapu's simple but powerful messages on the whale shark are recalled fondly even today. 'The whale shark is like a guest to our shores. *Atithi devo bhava* (Guests are like god),' he exhorted his audiences.

'These sharks come to Gujarat to breed, so we are like their parents. Each of them is like our daughter who has come back to her parent's home, to give birth to her child. We should protect our daughter, take care of her. Isn't that what we do in our homes?' This was heartfelt communication, worthy of a standing ovation.

It was also the first time that a religious leader had taken up the cause of wildlife conservation in India. His spontaneous connection with the audience might indicate that this is a viable model to promote other wildlife conservation efforts across the country.

To help reinforce these positive messages about the whale shark, we also had to give it a new local name. The existing name 'barrel' sounded so poor and negative for such a magnificent creature. Once again, we put on our thinking caps. We decided to locally rename it 'vhali', which is phonetically close enough to 'whale' and means 'a dear one' in Gujarati, therefore naturally reminding people of the daughter analogy used by Morari Bapu.

We now had to make vhali a visible mascot of the campaign, a buzz had to be generated across Okhamandal. A life-sized inflatable balloon of vhali was carried to the coastal towns, drawing large crowds and building awareness about this gentle giant. Street plays were staged, where the story of a daughter coming home was used once again, to great effect. The campaign to save whale sharks gathered further momentum with groups of fishermen and all other stakeholders making public pledges not to kill them. Newspapers also carried prominent reports of this campaign.

We persuaded several towns on the Dwarka and Porbandar coastal stretches of Gujarat to adopt vhali the whale shark as their mascot. In fact, the pull of the campaign was strong enough to convince Ahmedabad, a city in interior Gujarat located miles away from whale sharks, to make vhali its mascot.

The results of this multi-pronged campaign began as a trickle and turned into a torrent. The first signals appeared when a few fishermen were found releasing whale sharks that had got entangled in their nets, despite the loss of opportunity and the cost involved in cutting their nets. This was reported in many leading newspapers.

The good deeds of such fishermen were recognized and applauded. The number of times whale sharks were killed came down steadily, and have fallen dramatically in recent years. Many more fishermen have realized the need to protect this species. Financial incentives for releasing whale sharks were also devised, particularly to defray the cost of repairing fishing nets.

The whale shark project was selected for the Green Governance Award in 2005, awarded by the prime minister of India. The project was also showcased at the International Whale Shark Conference held in Perth, Australia, in the same year. We were delighted that we could play a small role in helping save the largest fish on earth, an endangered species, from extinction.

Tata Chemicals has taken this project into the second phase now. The company, through TCSRD, is supporting research into ecological information about the whale shark and its migration patterns. When this information is disseminated to all the stakeholders, we hope it will lead to the development of better species management plans.

Vivek Talwar concludes his story by playing a video of a whale shark peacefully gliding through deep blue waters, set to gentle music. It is difficult to not feel overwhelmed.

Giving back to the community

The short tales told above—the dreamers of Tupni, the weavers of Okhai and vhali the gentle whale shark—form a small part of a large and beautiful canvas that Tata Chemicals is attempting to paint at all its locations across the world. Other parts of this canvas include efforts at empowering women, establishing the region's first rural business process outsourcing (BPO) unit to provide employment to locals and promoting rural entrepreneurship. All these initiatives are about giving people opportunities to create brighter futures for themselves.

It is particularly interesting and relevant to see that many of these community initiatives have no direct link with the business of the company, its growth or its profits. For instance, saving an endangered species such as the whale shark or promoting the local handicraft of Okhamandal is unlikely to contribute to the financial prosperity of Tata Chemicals. It is also encouraging to see at close quarters that such wide-ranging development of the community is now a thought deeply embedded in the organization. R. Mukundan, the current managing director of Tata Chemicals, writes in his annual message of 2011 to TCSRD, 'I am happy to say that objectives of social responsibility are equally well entrenched in the minds of our employees.'

However, there will always be lingering questions.

An environmentalist may well ask: Does a chemicals company such as this not impose costs on its environment far in excess of the benefits that these community initiatives deliver? In the name of industrialization and employment, is the fragile ecosystem of the Okhamandal region not being damaged by new industrial plants coming up in that area?

A shareholder may ask: Are the costs incurred on developing Okhai or saving the whale shark of any value to the company, given that these projects address the wider population and environment, and not the workforce or the immediate community of Tata Chemicals? Ratan Tata once observed that many people often wonder whether this is baggage that Tata companies can afford to carry.

An employee may also ask: Should these resources not be

allocated to making our own lives and futures more comfortable in the first instance, since the company profits from our hard work? Why should such care be taken of villages that are at some distance from our factory and women who play no role in our business?

Without attempting to answer these questions in detail, I want to only say that the philosophy of giving back to the community generously has been a legacy of the founders of the Tata Group, beginning with Jamsetji Tata. The efforts of Tata Chemicals and TCSRD, and indeed other Tata companies as well, represent a perpetuation of this noble philosophy for simple reasons that are good, honest and sincere.

Future tales of Okhamandal

Alka Talwar is immensely proud of what her company and TCSRD team have achieved. She talks of many challenges ahead in creating sustainable community ventures. She is, however, determined to reach the commitment that TCSRD has made, of reaching out to one million people by 2015. Surely there will be many interesting tales there.

But here is the story Alka narrates with most pride:

> Sometime ago, we had a public hearing regarding a proposed Tata Chemicals power plant project, scheduled to come up in the Mithapur area. A few NGOs and others turned up at this hearing, and made observations very critical of the project and some issues it may cause. At that point, some villagers stood up spontaneously and said: 'Tata Chemicals are our neighbours. We have had an ongoing relationship with them for many years. They are our partners. Of course, like all neighbours, we have ongoing issues with them, but we will speak to them and resolve all those matters. They have always been good to us.'

The Tribulations of
Tata Finance

*'Our greatest glory is not in never failing, but in rising up every
time we fail.'*

—Ralph Waldo Emerson

*'It takes a lot of trust to be appointed a leader. I see greatness of
character in this admission that once in a while things will and do
go wrong. Don't push them under the carpet. Deal with them.
Very few large corporations in India do this in practice.'*

—R. Gopalakrishnan, executive director,
Tata Sons Ltd

A letter arrives

Legend has it that, nearly 500 years ago, on 31 October 1517, a
letter signed by the German monk Martin Luther was pinned
to a church door in Wittenberg. It had far-reaching
consequences in the Christian world.

Nearer home, and much closer in time, a letter dated
12 April 2001, written by a person who called himself Shankar
Sharma, reached the desks of several important and influential
people in Mumbai. It had a similar dramatic impact in the
Tata world.

The recipients of the letter included the directors of Tata Finance Limited, India's stock market regulator, the Securities and Exchange Board of India (SEBI), and several leading newspapers. It levelled several allegations against Tata Finance and its erstwhile managing director, Dilip Pendse. It charged that a prospectus issued by the company, for a rights issue of preference shares, contained falsified information. It also alleged that a fraud had been committed in the company.

Most people who read the news, including myself, reacted with disbelief. How could a document issued by a Tata organization contain false information? Was it conceivable that a major fraud could be committed by a managing director of a company that was part of this respected corporate house? This is the shocking tale of how things went terribly wrong in Tata Finance. It is also the story of how the Tata Group acknowledged and dealt with the whole affair, establishing, in the process, new standards of corporate governance in the country.

Dreaming big

Tata Finance Limited was a company with big ambitions. It had grown rapidly in the late 1990s, branching out into several areas of financial services. These included the hire and purchase of commercial vehicles and the financing of cars and consumer durables. The company accepted fixed deposits from members of the public, providing them a good rate of interest in return. It was planning to enter merchant banking, securities trading and other financial advisory services. Dilip Pendse, the managing director, was the chief architect of many of these plans.

Within the company there were dreams of glitzy offices that would rival those in the financial nerve centres of Canary

Wharf, London and Wall Street, New York. A magnificent building in the Fort office district of Mumbai had been purchased, to serve as the future corporate headquarters. Young team members would often imagine how this building would eventually look—with handsome brass plates, busily flashing trading screens and hundreds of consumers walking in every day to buy or sell stock, invest in deposits or apply for loans. This would be a one-stop financial services shop, the likes of which India had never seen before.

Tata Finance also established a housing finance subsidiary, called Tata Homefinance Limited. It structured tie-ups with leading manufacturers and marketers of vehicles. A joint venture company was formed for rendering foreign exchange services in India. The company was clearly exploring growth through multiple opportunities including strategic alliances, and it was pursuing this with speed.

Grand events symbolized these ambitions quite vividly. One occasion was the launch of Tata Finance–American Express co-branded credit cards that was held on the terrace of the exclusive Chambers in the Taj Mahal Hotel at Mumbai, in December 2000. In full view of the splendid Gateway of India, the sparkling Arabian Sea and the majestic central dome of the Taj, the card was launched with much fanfare as yet another milestone on the company's pathway to heaven.

No one could have imagined that beneath this bright visage flowed a murky current. Until the moment the shocking letter from the man who called himself Shankar Sharma arrived.

Shock, introspection and determination

In an article on this subject published by Tata Group Publications, appropriately titled 'Grime and Salvation', Ishaat Hussain, finance director of Tata Sons, says: 'That letter alerted us, and further investigations revealed that there had indeed been some serious irregularities.' He goes on to add, 'We were all taken aback.'

After an initial denial of the allegations by the Tata Finance management, it soon became clear that the letter was a case where smoke indicated a raging fire. The predominant mood in Bombay House, headquarters of the Tata Group, was one of dismay and anger at what had happened, but there was also a realization that dealing with this matter openly and transparently was the most important thing to do now. There was a sense of extreme urgency, and Tata Finance occupied the mind space of several senior directors of Tata Sons.

Meanwhile, it became painfully clear that Tata Finance had become almost insolvent. It had borrowings of about Rs 2700 crore, a huge figure by any standard. Of this, Rs 875 crore represented money belonging to four lakh small depositors. For many of these depositors, these were savings of an entire lifetime, funds kept aside for retirements, children's marriages and medical emergencies. They had trusted Tata Finance with these funds primarily because of the Tata name and, now, Tata Finance was not in a position to repay these depositors. There could not have been a worse moment in the history of a financial corporation.

How had this situation come to pass? The detailed events leading to this debacle can perhaps be the subject of an entire book, filled with many plots and sub-plots. Yet the key story, which was rapidly unfolding, was as follows: Tata Finance, led by Dilip Pendse, had lent approximately Rs 525 crore to some of its own subsidiary companies and affiliates, including a company called Nishkalp. A large part of that money had been invested in the stock market, in scrips of poor and speculative quality. Later investigations by the company revealed that many of these stock transactions were carried out to secure personal profits. When these scrips came crashing down, the original investments vanished and only a gaping black hole remained, with nowhere to hide.

In the midst of this tense and unfortunate situation, the chairman of Tata Sons, Ratan Tata, clearly defined two principles which would guide action. First and foremost, the interests of every depositor would be fully protected, so that no one who had trusted the Tata name lost on account of these ill-advised actions by some members of the Tata Finance management. Second, a thorough investigation would be completed, so that the guilty could be legally pursued and punished.

Ishaat Hussain says in 'Grime and Salvation', 'Mr Tata recommended to the Tata Sons board that they stand behind the company and make available funds to meet all its financial commitments, and the board fully endorsed this.'

Magnitude and speed of response

Pause here for a moment, dear reader. Reflect on the fact that Tata Sons Limited could have merely adhered to its limited legal responsibilities, rather than be determined to meet all the financial liabilities of Tata Finance. Also, consider that the quantum of funds required to do this was very significant. Arranging for such an amount at short notice posed challenges of feasibility, logistics and much else. Where would the funds come from? Who would be responsible for raising the full amount? How would the monies be returned to individual depositors across the length and breadth of the country, wherever required?

Yet, this was not merely the chosen path; it was the

spontaneously chosen path. Having observed decision-making in the Tata Group for over two decades now, I am convinced that any option that did not meet these basic principles of honesty and fairness would have been peremptorily tossed into the dustbin. Therefore, the way forward was proposed and adopted quite unanimously.

On 25 July 2001, an extraordinary public statement was issued, candidly admitting that Tata Finance was in distress as a result of a fraud committed upon it, and the Tatas would ensure that no depositor lost any money.

The Tata Group, working through two holding companies, Tata Sons and Tata Industries, provided Tata Finance with cash and corporate guarantees amounting to Rs 615 crore. This was an unprecedented event in Indian corporate history. These funds would be available to repay all creditors, as and when required. So every depositor could sleep peacefully, knowing that his or her funds were absolutely safe.

The non-flying helicopter

In the offices of Tata Finance, Ratan Tata's instructions infused fresh energy and life.

At a meeting held among key employees in the corporate headquarters, a clear decision was communicated: no depositor who wanted his money should ever be turned away, even for a single moment, without his money. Detailed plans were made to implement this decision, covering every town and every branch of Tata Finance across the country. The entire company was put into execution mode.

A small story illustrates the determination with which the team responded to the crisis. Everyone knew that if nervous depositors came to the offices of Tata Finance asking for their funds, a speedy response was critical. Therefore, it was even decided to keep a helicopter on standby so that funds could be transported quickly by air, if necessary. The team felt proud to be part of a Tata company, and wanted to ensure that people were not let down, whatever the cost or effort.

The helicopter was not used at all, though it may have added some excitement to these proceedings and also provided Indian television channels a few dramatic visuals. All these elaborate arrangements were rendered entirely redundant—such was the trust in the Tata name and the reassurance provided by the company, that only a handful of the four lakh small depositors withdrew their money. There was no run on the bank, not even the faint beginnings of one, despite the public statement and everyone knowing about the huge losses that had been incurred.

An investor named Luis De Menezes wrote to the *Indian Express* during those days, and a paragraph from his letter captures the prevailing sentiment well:

> Even after the scam [how former Managing Director Dilip Pendse helped run up huge losses], I have not thought of withdrawing my fixed deposit from there. At least for me, Tata Finance is the only trustworthy NBFC left in which I can deposit my money and have sound sleep. The culprits involved in this scam should be brought to book and also sued for tarnishing the Tata name.

I had myself held a fixed deposit in Tata Finance in those days, and the thought of withdrawing it did not even occur for a single moment, the simple reason being that I instinctively knew it would be absolutely safe, even though I wasn't privy to the discussions of those days.

Pursuing the culprits

Getting to the bottom of the entire affair and bringing the culprits to book was the second principle that Ratan Tata had laid down for dealing with this episode. This was important in all such cases, not merely to resolve the issue at hand and to ensure that the guilty were punished but also to throw up important lessons and changes required for the future.

The episode of Nick Leeson, financial whiz-kid turned rogue trader at the Barings Bank, comes readily to mind. By indulging in unauthorized trades and hiding losses from his superiors who considered him a financial rock star, he lost an unbelievable sum of US$1.3 billion. These losses were more than the entire capital and reserves of the bank, and therefore effectively wiped out a 230-year-old institution. Barings had been considered infallible and had served as bankers to the Queen herself. Now, it all came crumbling down. Leeson was arrested, extradited to Singapore where the crimes had been committed, and sentenced to six and half years in prison.

More importantly, the investigation of this collapse immediately threw up important lessons in internal controls, sound monitoring, risk assessment and risk management. Many international banks quickly took these lessons on board, and made the necessary changes in their processes and structures. These remedial actions are unlikely to entirely prevent all future attempts at fraud, since highly intelligent and equally crooked human beings will always find new ways to beat the best processes and controls. But the measures resulting from the investigation will certainly help reduce the probability of their occurrence.

In a similar fashion, Tata Finance launched its own investigation, and then moved forward to initiate legal action against those found guilty in the affair. Here is yet another excerpt from 'Grime and Salvation' that summarizes the steps that were then implemented expeditiously:

> The internal team and external investigators also evaluated available documents and built up a paper trail. In the first week of August, based on legal advice from an eminent criminal lawyer and a report from an independent chartered accountant, Tata Finance and Tata Industries filed an FIR (first information report) with the Economic Offences Wing, Mumbai Police, against Mr Pendse and certain former Tata Finance employees.
>
> But matters were not to end here.
>
> 'We moved the courts when the Mumbai Police filed a closure report with respect to our complaints,' says Mr Hussain. 'We took the stance that we will not let go the culprits. We moved the Bombay High Court and got the investigation transferred to the Central Bureau of Investigation. In the Supreme Court, too, our stand was vindicated. Six criminal complaints were filed in all, including three with the Delhi Police, and six complaints with SEBI for violation of various securities laws.
>
> 'Dilip Pendse was charge-sheeted in two complaints, and taken into judicial custody.'

These actions showcase the admirable resolve of the Tata Group, to deal firmly and summarily with any subversion of the value systems that Tata stands for. However, there were also some systemic errors and failures to be dealt with to guard against the recurrence of such episodes.

Matters of corporate governance

The eminent Irish novelist James Joyce once said, 'A man's errors are his portals of discovery.' Stepping through the unfortunate portals of the Tata Finance episode, the most obvious discovery is that no institution is above error or poor judgement, not even one as reputed as the Tata Group.

While the directors of Tata Finance resigned, taking constructive moral responsibility for this extraordinary lapse, many questions of governance remained to be addressed. Where had the checks and balances failed? Why had no whistleblower come forward to reveal the fraud much earlier in the day? Why did they keep quiet, until the surfacing of the Shankar Sharma letter? Did the board of directors of Tata Finance discharge its responsibilities with the independence and oversight required of it?

Clearly, there were shortcomings in many of these areas of corporate governance, and therefore many lessons to be learnt. The Tata Group has, since then, put in place several processes to strengthen these systems of governance, which are the backbone of any institution. Some of these are statutory requirements, and others are crafted specifically by the Tata organization. Here are some important examples.

Chief financial officers of Tata enterprises now no longer report only to the managing directors of their respective companies. They also have a line of reporting to Bombay House, where the finance director of Tata Sons is based. This dual structure of reporting ensures not merely review of key data and financial information at multiple levels but also opens channels of communication that are invaluable to the governance process, at the seniormost levels of the organization.

Similarly, the chief internal auditor reports to the chairman of the Audit Committee of the board of directors, who is an independent director with expertise in matters of finance, accounting and controls. He is not aligned with the promoters and is not a member of the company's management either. This helps ensure sharp, expert and independent oversight of a critical watchdog function, which is charged with highlighting deviations and lapses.

The Tata Group has also put in place a written code to prevent insider trading. There is also a policy to encourage whistleblowers to come forward and report ethical or other important concerns.

Boards of directors have also become much more accountable, not merely for performance but also for good governance. There is increasing consciousness that, at this high table, they are protectors of the company, its brand name and legacy. They have to shoulder an increasingly weighty burden on this front as companies become larger, wealthier, more complex and widespread in their operations.

These are good lessons arising from a particularly painful episode. But there is another area, even more important, that is essential to reflect on. It is the subject of values and culture, in ensuring good corporate governance.

Values and integrity

Every institution has a set of publicly stated beliefs and value systems. These are put up on soft boards and notice boards in our offices, where we see them every day. But, as a human resources head in a large Tata company told me during the writing of this book, the truth is that every employee does not necessarily put into practice all these values. Companies have to live with this mix of people. Therefore, companies have to ensure that they spot the 100 per cent practitioners who truly believe in all these stated values, and rely on them to lead the organization. This is very important, because in moments of great temptation or crisis, these values are inevitably put to the test.

Noshir Soonawala, one of the most respected senior leaders in the Tata Group, emphasizes that the need to maintain values, principles and character at all levels is paramount. He points out that maintaining principles on every tier, in all dealings, across so many businesses and so many people will become even more challenging as the Tata Group continues to grow and expand dramatically. He views this as one of the foremost challenges for the future.

Here is how Ishaat Hussain sums up this challenge:

> Good governance is the lifeblood of every reputed organization. Of course this requires strong processes and vigilant boards of directors, but most importantly it requires professional integrity on the part of senior executives. We have to bear this in mind while selecting our chief executive officers, chief financial officers and their counterparts, in the future. If they are unscrupulous and, particularly, if they gang up together, they can drive coaches and horses through the system.

The reincarnation of Tata Finance

The story of Tata Finance does not end here. At walking distance from Bombay House, in a stately looking building called 'One Forbes', are the elegant corporate offices of a relatively new company called Tata Capital. The company, established in September 2007, promises consumers that it will do just what is right for them. It offers a suite of financial services including consumer loans, investment services, commercial finance, investment banking, securities, travel and forex services, credit cards—in fact, products and services which are identical to the dreams that Tata Finance once had.

With strong systems of governance and decision-making, a vigilant senior management and board, the company is well on its way to making a big and positive impact in the world of finance. The decisions that the Tata Group implemented several years ago during the Tata Finance crisis are a strong foundation on which Tata Capital has now been built.

In the final analysis, public trust in the Tata brand has only been enhanced by the transparent, upright handling of that crisis. To err is human. It is the organization's response to an error committed, in one of the constituent parts in this case, that severely tests principles and character.

The identity of Shankar Sharma

Finally, who is Shankar Sharma, the man who wrote the letter alleging that fraud had been committed in Tata Finance? Was he an outsider who had gained access to information, or was he an insider who wanted to alert the Tata Group and others to wrongdoings within the company?

More than a decade later, his identity remains unknown and mysterious. He perhaps had the best interests of the company at heart, and the corporate world will need many more people like him. His letter certainly made its impact. However, this story can be complete in all respects only after a conversation with him. So, I wonder, will he ever reveal himself?

Tanishq Sets the Gold Standard

'Courage is not simply one of the virtues, but the form of every virtue at the testing point.'

—C.S. Lewis, *The Unquiet Grave*

'Belief in the Indian consumer opportunity was the source of our courage.'

—Bhaskar Bhat, managing director,
Titan Industries Limited

Tanishq almost shuts shop

Clara Lobo manages the beautiful Tanishq showroom on Turner Road, a busy high street in the upscale Bandra area of Mumbai. Inside the store, a family is buying gold jewellery for their daughter's wedding in a few weeks' time. A young couple has just walked in to look at engagement rings. Saleswomen, dressed in elegant brown sarees, are navigating the couple through an assortment of styles. At another counter, two women look visibly excited while making a selection of a set of diamond-studded bangles. Soft music plays in the background. Lobo explains to me how the scenario has changed.

All Indian women want to own Tanishq jewellery today. Our brand has connected so well with them. We have the happiest customers in the world. But it was so different when we began, for many years. I joined Tanishq fifteen years ago, in 1997, just a year after the brand had been launched. We would wait for hours together for a single customer to walk in. Often, a whole week would pass by in silence, and we would feel very depressed. Our performance was so poor that sometimes we even heard that this brand would be shut down.

Two thousand kilometres from Lobo's store, in the garden city of Bangalore, sits Xerxes Desai, the man who founded Tanishq. Now retired, he speaks slowly but clearly in his refined Oxford accent.

Yes, for some years there certainly was pressure to hive off this business. There was mixed support from some people in the Tatas. There was also an opinion that the jewellery business could only be run by family jewellers, that it never could be corporatized.

But I was firm in my view, and I said that any such hiving off or closure would happen over my dead body. We saw the huge opportunity, we had belief and we persisted.

Tanishq is the largest and most successful brand of jewellery in India today, serving nearly a million people (mostly women) each year and generating annual revenues of approximately Rs 10,000 crore, making it one of the glittering jewels in the Tata crown. It is a much-celebrated success that is steadily transforming the second largest consumer sector in the country. In terms of sheer size, only the food industry beats jewellery.

This is the story of Tanishq, the vision and courage that powered it, and how it overcame all its early errors and struggles to set the gold standard for India.

Wristwatches and jewellery

Titan Industries, the company which launched Tanishq, was founded in 1984 as a joint venture between the Tata Group and the government of Tamil Nadu. In April 1987, it launched Titan watches in India. Built on the back of quartz technology and a range of fabulous designs, these watches took the market by storm.

Within a few years, Titan had established a formidable market share of more than 50 per cent in the organized market, frequently walking away with awards for superlative marketing. Titan had become a household name in the country. Even the first movement of Mozart's Twenty-Fifth Symphony, which Titan used in much of its advertising, became as popular as Bollywood songs in many Indian households. Given that very few Indians have any interest in Western classical music, this was a spectacular achievement by itself. Here was a brand that could do no wrong.

Desai, a long-time Tata veteran who founded the company and became its first managing director, recalls, 'Titan was doing extraordinarily well in the market. Sales volumes of our watches were jumping far beyond initial expectations. We revelled in our success.'

At that stage, Titan Industries entered the jewellery business for reasons that could be termed unconventional. In 1991 India faced a serious problem when its foreign currency reserves were severely depleted. The Government of India had to pledge several hundred tonnes of gold from its national reserves to help resolve that crisis. It is ironic that a jewellery business that today uses hundreds of tonnes of gold each year was born at that exact moment.

Titan used many imported components in its watches, even as it rapidly ramped up indigenous production, and the cash-strapped government insisted that it earn foreign exchange to fund these imports. The company was therefore on the lookout for a suitable project that could earn foreign currency through exports.

Desai says, with a mischievous smile, 'We looked at several other ventures before we finally chose to make and export jewellery. For instance, a granite business was actively considered for several weeks, before it was dropped. Indian granite was in huge demand those days for making Japanese tombstones. Fortunately for us, that bizarre idea was speedily buried in its own graveyard.'

The reasons for choosing to pursue the jewellery business were quite simple. World over, at the premium end of the market, jewellers were also watchmakers, and vice versa. Both watches and jewellery were objects of exquisite design and personal adornment. The same stores retailed both in Europe and America. And both participated in the same exhibitions worldwide.

So, Titan Industries invested in a factory and the expertise for manufacturing jewellery. The plant was established in Hosur, an industrial town in Tamil Nadu, at a distance of approximately forty kilometres from Bangalore. It was also in close proximity to the original unit that manufactured wristwatches. Beautifully landscaped and designed, the factory looked as sublime as the jewellery it would make.

Since the objective was to export all this jewellery and earn foreign exchange, the initial designs that were created in this factory were entirely Western and European in their inspiration. European designers were hired to achieve this. Jewelled watches were also created. However, two things happened soon thereafter that created immediate uncertainty for the viability of the project.

The demand patterns for gold jewellery in Europe and the United States changed dramatically. Due to a global economic downturn, the ostentatious spending of the Thatcher–Reagan era gave way to a new austerity, and women moved towards the more inexpensive steel-and-gold looks. Titan's fine jewellery was just not competitive enough in this new reality. It seemed that the export game was not worth the candle.

With the onset of the 1991 reforms the Indian economy recovered to a remarkable degree a year later. Other industries such as IT built large export surpluses. Imports were freely permitted, and the need to earn foreign exchange through exports disappeared. Suddenly, for Titan, selling jewellery to Europe was no longer essential.

Desai continues:

> So, here we had a big jewellery factory, and no overseas market worth the effort of developing. This was an expensive plant, with expensive people. The European market for gold jewellery had shrunk, demand from those quarters had declined and it no longer made sense to compete in that space. That is when we turned to the Indian market, and thought of Tanishq.

The birth of Tanishq

Xerxes Desai had also spoken to J.R.D. Tata in the initial exploratory phases, and sought his views on entering the Indian jewellery market. JRD, who was in his final years as chairman of the Tata Group, was almost childishly excited by the prospect, and quite positive in his response.

'There's a very big market in India for jewellery,' JRD said. 'Given our technical skills and reputation, we should be able to do well.'

But JRD left the final decision to the managing director of

the company, like he always did. 'He would hardly ever say no,' Desai recalls, 'unless it was something that he felt was not ethically or morally correct. Only then would he tell me: "Xerxes, in the Tatas we don't do it that way."'

Jamshed Bhabha, a senior Tata director on Titan's board, was even more vocal in his support for a jewellery business. He proudly showed Xerxes Desai a picture of his aunt, Lady Meherbai Tata, wife of Sir Dorab Tata, standing next to Queen Mary of England and wearing the monumental Jubilee diamond that weighed an amazing 245 carats (49.07 g). It was sold by the Tata family in the 1930s to Cartier, then on to Harry Winston, who sold it to a French billionaire, who in turn sold it to diamond czar Robert Mouawad, the current owner. Perhaps there was some fond hope that Titan's jewellery business, if it indeed began, would, some day, reclaim this coveted diamond for the Tatas!

While J.R.D. Tata's and Jamshed Bhabha's views were positive, this was not the response from other directors in the Tata Group. There was deep scepticism that jewellery, a trade that flourished in the unorganized sector, could ever be successful in the hands of a corporate body.

Ishaat Hussain, finance director of Tata Sons, has been a member of the board of directors of Titan Industries for more than two decades. He recalls, 'Jewellery stores in India had always worked with the owner/proprietor model, where the owner knows each customer and builds close personal contact with clients and their families. It was difficult to imagine at that time that this model could be corporatized, that it could change so fast.'

Within Titan too, there were several pockets of cynicism, particularly within the prosperous watches business. Why venture into an unknown industry, when Titan watches were performing so splendidly? Wouldn't it make far more sense to strengthen the watches portfolio by adding new brands or markets, which could further enhance its success?

It is in such moments that the mettle of leadership is tested. Desai reflected on these views calmly, and also discussed them with his senior team, but time and again one indisputable fact leapt out at him. The Indian appetite for jewellery was huge— the size of the market exceeded Rs 50,000 crore annually (today, it is closer to three times that size). The opportunity was too enormous to ignore. Titan's proven manufacturing, marketing and design skills, and its Tata parentage, could be leveraged to crack open this market. Yes, it would not be a cakewalk like the watches business has been, but the rewards in time to come were worth the likely struggles of the initial years, as Tanishq sought to change consumer behaviour and loyalty to the 'family jeweller'.

Leaders of nations and large businesses have to often make lonely decisions, and Desai did, encouraged by the enthusiasm of those who led the jewellery project. In 1996, he decided to launch the first retail showroom of Tanishq in India.

Even as he took this call, he may have looked one last time at a colourful painting of a *bindu*, by the famous Indian artist Syed Haider Raza, which hung in the offices of Titan. The bindu is a dot, which is the source of all energy. Xerxes Desai's decision was on the dot, and here the source of his energy was his belief in the Indian consumer.

Naming the baby

Marketers spend enormous time trying to create a new brand name. They commission quantitative and qualitative consumer research studies. They appoint experts to analyse the subliminal messages that a brand name conveys. They do many other things that supposedly convey scientific rigour in this area.

However, history tells us that the best brand names are often not born in this way. They just need to have a nice, catchy ring to them, an authentic origin and, if possible, a simple meaning as well. The name Tata is a good illustration: it is the family name of the founder of the group. Similarly, the brand name Apple was chosen because Steve Jobs worked in an apple farm one summer and it came before Atari (a competitor) in the phone book.

The name Tanishq, chosen by Desai and acknowledged today as a masterstroke by everyone, has a similar history. Here is his own version of the story:

Anil Manchanda [who was leading the jewellery project in the company] was keen on the name Aurum. But this would look like a piece of the periodic table, and no one would really understand it, so we said no. We had previously used the brand name Celeste in the European market, during the early days of jewellery export. But we soon realized that Celeste had already been trademarked by another company.

So, I thought of the word Tanishq. I was clear that the word should possess a feminine and Indian feel to it. It would also be useful for the names of our two promoters to be reflected in the name. So, *ta* stands both for Tata and Tamil Nadu, the promoters of our company. And *nishq* means a piece of jewellery. The name sounded even better when Fali Vakeel of our advertising agency, Lintas, pointed out to me that Tanishq, when sliced differently, is a combination of *tan* (body) and *ishq* (love). These are words which go very well with jewellery.

But what is really interesting is how the name Tanishq jumped into my mind at the very beginning. I am fond of dogs, and I owned a Harlequin Great Dane at that time, called Monishqa. Also, the young daughter of a close friend, whose brains we had picked in the early days when working on Titan's marketing strategy, was named Monisha. So, I used these names often, and I think they triggered Tanishq, which sounds quite similar! When I tossed it around in my mind after that, it sounded very poetic and beautiful.

Marketers may wish to bear this story in mind when they commission research firms to search for brand names.

An Indian summer

Tanishq was launched in India in 1996, as a brand of precious gem set (studded) jewellery. Plain gold jewellery was a very small part of the product offering. As Desai mentioned in a speech many years later, the idea was to make Tanishq 'a composite Indian avatar of Cartier, Tiffany, Asprey and even Ernest Jones all rolled into one'.

Bhaskar Bhat, the current managing director of Titan Industries, explains why this choice was made:

> Plain gold jewellery offers little opportunity for differentiation (or so we felt at that time). With everyone sourcing from the same pool of *karigars* (artisans), new designs are quickly copied. Also, everyone knows the price of gold. The customer then adds labour and wastage charges, and establishes the base price, leaving the jeweller with no pricing power. You make money by focusing on volumes and faster inventory turns.
>
> Studded jewellery is a different story altogether. Customers don't really know how to accurately value gems. Even with diamonds, where we have a clear evaluation process based on the four Cs of cut, colour, clarity and caratage, it is not easy to peg down a price. There is also the opportunity to be innovative in design, since people are less likely to copy them, given the low volumes. As a result, the jeweller has more price flexibility, and margins are much higher in studded jewellery.

The decision to get primarily into studded jewellery created a constraint because it meant that Tanishq could not offer any significant variety in 22 carat gold to consumers, despite this caratage being the standard in the Indian market. Eighteen carat gold would have to be used to make Tanishq jewellery, since 22 carat gold is too soft to hold diamonds or other gemstones. Simultaneously, there was also an effort to move the market for plain gold jewellery to 18 carat, with the belief that this offering would enable consumers to spread their budgets over larger or more pieces, since 18 carat gold is less expensive than 22 carat gold. It would also benefit customers because 18 carat gold is more scratch-proof and dent-proof.

The company knew that by doing this it was taking on the risk of trying to change long-standing consumer behaviour. Moving consumers from 22 carat gold to 18 carat jewellery was fundamental to the success of this strategy. However, Desai and team were supremely confident. They had successfully transformed the watches market. They were inspired marketers, recognized repeatedly as the best in the land. There was no reason to doubt that they would not do it again.

In July 1996, the first Tanishq showroom opened for business at Cathedral Road in Chennai. The showroom looked like a highly exclusive five-star hotel. Fitted with green marble, low counters, works of art and some show windows, there was very little jewellery on display compared to other Indian jewellery stores. Staff was hired and trained extensively in the art of customer service. An advertisement campaign was launched with a view to create mystery around the brand and also communicate that the showrooms were as precious as the Tanishq jewellery itself. Now the only thing that needed to happen was for customers to walk in. So they waited . . .

The Indian woman remained totally unmoved.

Gold jewellery was not merely a piece of adornment for her; it was her personal wealth, traditionally called *stridhan*. She was not willing to dilute this important aspect of her life by buying 18 carat gold, which was, in her perception, far less valuable than 22 carat gold. In her view, 'less than precious' 18 carat jewellery was eminently unsuitable, particularly for precious occasions such as weddings and Indian festivals. The few women who overcame this adverse perception and stepped into Tanishq showrooms were promptly intimidated by the opulent surroundings and the Western-style jewellery. 'Not for me' was the most common reaction, which did not change even after several months of intense marketing efforts.

With a bang and a thud, the marketers who could do no wrong were brought down to earth. The expensive jewellery factory in Hosur continued to incur losses, because there was little being sold. Tanishq was in distress.

When it rains, it pours

During the period 1996 to 2000, even as Tanishq was failing miserably to attract consumers, the parent company, Titan Industries, suffered many other setbacks as well.

The watches business made a foray into Europe, which turned out to be a misadventure. The losses incurred on this account ran into more than Rs 150 crore, which was a huge amount for the company to bear. A relatively new business in table clocks and wall clocks had to be discontinued, because its potential size and profitability was not attractive enough. The clocks bore the stamp of beautiful design, and the few remaining pieces are still sought after by connoisseurs, but the financial returns were completely inadequate. In addition, the company had invested in a joint venture with Timex Watches of the

USA, which was also running into major financial and operational challenges.

Bhaskar Bhat recalls, 'We were deep in debt. Our initial successes in the watches market had given us an aura of invincibility, which was now peeling away. Media speculated that we would sell the jewellery business. Some reports even said that the Tata Group was very unhappy with our entry into this sector. The going was getting really rough.'

Indeed, there were several frowns and worried faces whenever the future of the jewellery business came up for discussion. It had already lost more than Rs 100 crore. Some observers reckoned that the brand was stuck in no man's land, and there was no light at the end of the tunnel. To make it worse, the company had to bear these huge losses at a time when nothing else seemed to be going well.

Desai also knew that the core watches business was earning much less money than originally planned, which is why the cash required to support the jewellery segment, on which the project and its borrowings were based, was rapidly evaporating. Several debates erupted now on the future of this business. Some of these debates occurred in Bombay House and were also thereafter tabled at the board of directors of Titan.

A protracted and sharply worded correspondence between Desai and Ishaat Hussain (who represented the Tata Group on Titan's board of directors) was typical of this period. Hussain was concerned about the mounting losses, and he took up the matter in no uncertain terms. The exchange of letters appeared to be veering into a deadlock.

Xerxes Desai says:

> Ishaat and I were good friends; in fact, my son had worked with him in earlier years. He was doing his job as a man of finance, but I entirely disagreed with his point of view on the

jewellery business. I was convinced the business had big potential; perhaps we had made errors in execution leading to the losses, but we could change that around.

There was also a view in some quarters in the Tatas and elsewhere that jewellery was not our core competence. These people said we were a watches company; that is why we were failing so badly in this new venture. But I ask you, if the Tatas had focused only on their core competence, wouldn't we have remained a textiles and trading group for the past century?

It is to the credit of the Tata Group that though there was significant impatience and discomfort with the jewellery business in the offices of Bombay House, they left the final decision to Desai and the board of directors of Titan Industries.

An interview with Ratan Tata, published in *Businessworld* magazine in December 2000, highlights this approach.

The interviewers, Tony Joseph and Radhika Dhawan, ask him if Titan had entered the jewellery business against the wishes of the group, and was then not delivering.

Ratan Tata responded, 'You referred to the case of Titan going into the jewellery business, and the GEO's [group executive office's] contrary view on this. Ideally, where is this kind of issue to be discussed and debated? At the boards of these companies.'

He went on to say that the boards of companies had to be more concerned with their businesses than they had been in the past, and that the CEO should take his directions from the board, which is the requisite authority.

Notwithstanding Ratan Tata's viewpoint, pressure mounted on Desai to hive off the jewellery business into a separate company that could be sold, if necessary. This was in essence an exit plan, and the Tata Group appeared to have lost faith in Tanishq. Within Titan Industries, there was indifferent support from many segments in the prosperous watches section, which considered the jewellery business a bottomless and useless sink for funds. However, there was strong support for Tanishq from the manufacturing unit, which had discovered a passion for making fine jewellery, the sales and marketing team of the jewellery business, directors representing the Tamil Nadu government and some senior Tata directors such as Jamshed Bhabha.

Desai again consulted his senior management team, which included Jacob Kurian, Vasant Nangia and Bhaskar Bhat. He then decided that he would take the pressure head-on—the consumer opportunity in jewellery was as large as ever, despite the initial lack of success and the current financial stress. The need of the hour was a sound consumer proposition and good execution, and then it was just a question of giving the venture the time to succeed.

Desai says his knowledge of the pioneering history of the Tata Group gave him the confidence to shut out the noise and march ahead.

Enter the karatmeter

Tanishq now made two big changes to its consumer offering. In 1999, bowing to the voice of the Indian woman, it abandoned its primary focus on 18 carat studded jewellery, and introduced a wide range of 22 carat gold jewellery. Many of these were designs inspired by an Indian look. This was built on a limited pilot offering of 22 carat jewellery that had already been launched. With this change in offering, many more Indian women opened their minds and wallets to Tanishq.

It also pioneered what will be remembered forever as one of the greatest innovations in the Indian jewellery market, the karatmeter. This machine used the science of spectroscopy to measure the purity or caratage of gold in three minutes. It did this using rays of specified frequency without destroying the piece of jewellery. Karatmeters were placed in Tanishq showrooms where customers could see them in operation. Now, the karatmeter could instantly certify the purity of the jewellery at the point of sale.

'This was a masterstroke by the team,' says Desai. 'An obscure scientific laboratory instrument suddenly became the touchstone of our age.'

Tanishq then launched an aggressive marketing campaign highlighting that a lot of the jewellery sold in India actually offered less caratage of gold than promised, enabling jewellers to cheat the consumer and make a quick buck in the bargain. The advertisements highlighted the impeccable quality and caratage of Tanishq, invoking the Tata tradition of trust and the modern quality controls it used. The advertisements also invited consumers to walk into Tanishq showrooms and check the purity of their gold jewellery on the karatmeter at no cost.

Within days, thousands of women had walked into Tanishq showrooms to check their jewellery, and over 60 per cent of them had found that their gold was well below the stated caratage. In other words, they had been cheated by their jewellers, whom they had trusted all along.

As news of this spread like wildfire, queues of women formed in front of Tanishq showrooms to check the purity of their gold. In many showrooms, including the early flagship store at Dickenson Road in Bangalore, many women broke down and wept inconsolably when they checked their gold on the karatmeter and saw that it was impure. This meant that their savings of a lifetime, much of which was in gold, diminished in value.

Tears gave way to rage and we all know hell hath no fury like a woman scorned (or cheated by her jeweller).

Such fury at family jewellers who cheat also translated into trust in Tanishq, which offered a written guarantee of 22 carat gold, backed by the Tata name and stringent quality controls.

C.K. Venkataraman, the current chief operating officer of the jewellery business, says that Tanishq has built on this promise of trust by not only offering the highest standards of purity in gold and diamonds, but also by being transparent with customers. 'Purity is concretely supported by the karatmeter, but you will find transparency in every bit of Tanishq,' he says, 'product, pricing, exchange policies, advertising—we take pride in being very clear and very customer friendly.'

Trust continues to remain the foremost consumer proposition of Tanishq.

Belief, focus and innovation

The introduction of 22 carat gold jewellery corrected an initial error of judgement, and the karatmeter had proved a game changer. But Tanishq was still seen by many women as too Western, too pricey and therefore 'not for me'. These remaining barriers had to be broken if the brand had to perform to potential.

In the year 2000, there was an unfortunate exodus of senior management from the stables of Tanishq. Vasant Nangia, the man who had introduced the karatmeter, and several members of his team, left to form their own jewellery retailing venture. Tanishq was still losing money. Into this vacuum stepped a new team headed by Jacob Kurian, who had worked with the Tata Group for over fifteen years.

The need of the hour was to infuse belief in the business and make it profitable. This would also mean convincing several lakh women that Tanishq was the best jewellery they could buy.

I had the good fortune of working as a senior member of Jacob's team in Tanishq during this phase of the business, before I eventually took charge from him as head of the business. Jacob was a charismatic leader who could never stand fools, and he relentlessly drove several waves of growth. He gathered a bunch of fine people around him and led them with rare energy, empathy and intellect. In those hectic days, we were a small team determined to make a big success of this business, and we were also aware that the sword of Damocles still hung somewhere from the ceiling.

Jacob infused belief in the future of Tanishq. One particular team event called 'I Believe' served to rally the troops by dramatically showcasing several reasons why Tanishq would succeed magnificently. It ended with all those present lighting candles in a dark conference hall, to reiterate their faith and confidence in the success of Tanishq.

From that period, three specific initiatives in the areas of marketing, financing and product innovation deserve mention here.

The first was was a gold jewellery exchange scheme called '19 = 22'. Women could bring in their gold jewellery and get it tested on the karatmeter. If the purity of their jewellery was lower than 22 carat and higher than 19 carat, they could exchange it for Tanishq's pure 22 carat jewellery of their choice, by paying only the manufacturing charges. The scheme again built on the karatmeter idea, and was a wild success. It resulted in several thousand women turning to Tanishq and away from their existing jewellers.

The second was the introduction of a new funding mechanism, by which gold for making jewellery could be procured on lease from international banks. Therefore, the need to invest hard cash in buying gold disappeared instantly, and Tanishq's working capital requirements came down significantly. This threw open the vistas for rapid growth, and was the second great innovation for Tanishq after the karatmeter.

The third was the creation and marketing of lightweight gold jewellery, which maximized the surface area of the piece but minimized the weight of gold used. This appealed greatly to budget-conscious women and also conveyed the key message that Tanishq was affordable.

Riding on the back of these initiatives, Tanishq crossed business revenues of Rs 500 crore by the year 2005. This was tremendous progress, as it marked a twenty-fold increase from the revenues of Rs 24 crore achieved in 1998. Most importantly, under Kurian's leadership, the business turned profitable. The Tata Group's senior management's conviction—lacking so far—went up significantly.

Hussain says his own view of the jewellery business was transformed by these developments. 'Tanishq was appealing to the mainstream now; the model now was quite different from the elitist 18 carat jewellery premise with which the business began. Execution was excellent, the karatmeter had made its point, and "gold on lease" was a game changer.'

An article titled 'Glittering Again', published on the Tata website in October 2003, now praised Tanishq as a trailblazer: 'Pioneering can be a poisoned chalice. Tanishq, as much a trailblazer in the jewellery industry as its parent Titan was in the watches industry, knows this better than most.'

The new face of Tanishq

An even more spectacular phase of growth began in the years thereafter. In 2002, Bhaskar Bhat had become the managing director of Titan Industries, and had defined economic success and consumer affection as the twin objectives of the company. In 2005, C.K. Venkataraman (Venkat) replaced me as the head of the jewellery business.

Venkat describes a magical moment of transformation:

> After a fundamental piece of consumer research, we understood that the evolving Indian woman has a new sense of self. She plays by the rules, but modifies them in a way which suits her. She seeks a harmonious coexistence between tradition and modernity. We seized on this insight to position Tanishq as a progressive Indian brand that combined tradition and heritage, a brand that offers new tales of tradition.

The brand had found its new face. The insight led to a coherent product strategy and several appealing advertising campaigns, which ushered in over half a million women into Tanishq showrooms. If the karatmeter had rescued the brand from failure, this new brand promise was a tipping point towards stupendous success.

Tanishq's first 'new tale of tradition' was a television film whose backdrop closely resembled the settings of a popular and award-winning Hindi film called *Parineeta*. In the film, a beautiful and very traditional Indian bride, bedecked in her fabulous Tanishq jewellery, goes out for a formal drive with her groom. When they are just out of sight of the family home, she quickly exchanges places with him, and gets into the driver's seat of the car with equal ease. The film appealed immediately to all Indian women who respect tradition, yet desire freedom and modernity.

Tanishq also emphasized its Indian heritage by designing jewellery for period Bollywood films such as *Paheli* and *Jodhaa Akbar*. In *Jodhaa Akbar*, a love story involving the famous Mughal emperor Akbar and the Rajput princess Jodhaa, Tanishq created not merely the jewellery for the royal couple, but also the jewelled armour and magnificent swords. It was a fabulous display of the craft of traditional jewellery. The brand simultaneously highlighted its modern appeal by creating distinctive crowns for winners of the glamorous Miss India contest.

Venkat also mentions Tanishq's assiduous efforts to woo the large Indian middle class, with schemes such as the Golden Harvest programme, where consumers could buy jewellery through advance instalments, with an attractive free instalment thrown in by the company. Several focused efforts went into targeting the wedding jewellery market, as well as the high-value jewellery segment.

Tanishq retail showrooms across India, managed for the most part by competent franchisees, offered consumers one of the best shopping experiences in the country. Rigorous retail workshops were conducted with these franchisees each year to ensure that each element of the brand's plans were fully in place. Venkat says the idea of these workshops was a seminal moment in the story of the brand, particularly since retail is all about detail.

Tanishq developed a new focus on transforming its customers into passionate fans of the brand. Thousands of women customers and their spouses were also invited to visit the jewellery factory at Hosur. Here, for the first time in their lives, they saw for themselves the process of jewellery making, and also held in their hands a ten kilogram ingot of pure Tanishq gold!

The brand also launched marketing campaigns to educate consumers about diamonds. In 2011, the legendary Bollywood actor Amitabh Bachchan paired up with his wife, Jaya Bachchan, in a memorable advertisement to showcase the virtues of diamonds marketed by Tanishq. Women responded by streaming into Tanishq stores, and sales of diamond jewellery shot up beyond expectations.

This was a dream run. Tanishq crossed annual revenues of Rs 5,000 crore with ease and hurtled towards its next big milestone. It also notched up rapid growth in profits. In his presentation at the Tata Group's Annual General Managers' Meeting (AGMM) in 2012, Ratan Tata highlighted the relative financial performance of various businesses in the group. All major Tata businesses were grouped into four performance quadrants, for ease of understanding. The jewellery business, which had virtually been written off a decade earlier, now featured in the topmost quadrant of profitability.

Transforming the jewellery industry

Behind the glamour of the Indian jewellery industry lie hidden some of the most primitive working conditions for the artisans who make handmade jewellery. They come from traditional jewellery-making areas and families, and their valuable skills are often passed on from one generation to the next. Yet, they have mostly worked in appallingly cramped conditions, exposed to heat, sweat, dust and hazardous chemicals. Because they are unorganized, they are exploited by crafty middlemen, who tend to pocket much of the profits, giving the artisans little in return. Readers of Charles Dickens's novels will find a lot of similarity between his descriptions of the poorest parts of London and the insides of these poorly lit jewellery workshops.

Tanishq, after achieving excellent growth and business

success, has now set about transforming these industry conditions. It has established 'karigar parks' that bring these artisans together and provide them with comfortable working conditions. Venkat says:

> We have an ambitious programme called Mr Perfect, which modernizes these facilities and injects respectability, prestige and glamour into the manufacturing of jewellery. From dingy workshops, we have created well-ventilated, clean environments that are comparable with modern offices. This will encourage artisans to happily remain in this profession for generations to come. We hope many more enlightened jewellers will follow in our wake.
>
> Jewellery always brings beautiful smiles to the faces of women. We want to bring equally broad smiles to the faces of the artisans who create these wonderful pieces with their own hands.

Bhaskar Bhat, the managing director of Titan Industries, speaks about the next phase of transformation that Tanishq should drive. The jewellery industry is often seen in poor light, he says, because of the perception that unaccounted or 'black' money is involved in large purchases. The government has recently initiated some action on this front, and Tanishq will once again be at the forefront of setting the right example. He says, 'Our vision is not merely to be a large and very successful player in jewellery, but to be an engine of transformation—only then can we be creators of wealth in the tradition of the Tatas.'

Looking back, looking ahead

In March 2012, Titan Industries hosted a gala dinner in the Taj Vivanta Hotel at Bangalore to celebrate twenty-five years of the company's existence. The board of directors, current and past members of senior management had turned up in strength. The dress code for the evening specified a touch of silver, but a number of elegant lady invitees chose to wear Tanishq gold and diamond jewellery instead.

Xerxes Desai, whose vision and courage had created Tanishq, was present. So was Ishaat Hussain, his friend from Tata headquarters, with whom he had debated the future of this business many years ago.

When Ishaat Hussain stood up to speak, he was gracious and aristocratic, as always. He said, 'On the jewellery business, I must admit that I was wrong. Xerxes' conviction has turned out to be quite right, and we must applaud him for having created such a magnificent enterprise.'

These are generous words, and they will do much to encourage future pioneers within the Tatas.

But Desai is not yet happy with Tanishq. He feels that while the brand may be a big commercial success, it will become iconic only if it sharpens its appeal and regains the high ground on design.

'Tanishq must segment the jewellery market based on designs and price points. It must go back to the design concept as a differentiator. A work of art is known by its concept, and jewellery is such an expansive art form. Look at what Faberge did with a blooming egg!'

Second Careers for Intelligent Women

'When both women and men bring their strengths to the workplace, business benefits.'

—Nancy Clark, CEO, Womensmedia Inc.

'Women should be encouraged to stay in the workforce. Many women would opt to keep working, if only companies offered more options, more flexibility.'

—Ruma Rao, human resources team, Tata Group

A proud woman at the cricket World Cup finals

On 2 April 2011, India won the cricket World Cup for only the second time in history, generating instant national euphoria. The venue was the Wankhede Stadium in Mumbai, and the din of the 45,000 spectators drowned out the sound of the waves lapping the shore of the Arabian Sea nearby. Standing in the midst of these joyous spectators, one woman felt very emotional for entirely different reasons.

Priyamvada Merchant, mother of two children and partner in a company called System Rex, felt as elated as the victorious Indian cricket team that night, because she knew she had won her own personal World Cup. The firm that she managed along with her business partner had created a very innovative underground drainage system at the stadium, using corrugated and perforated plastic pipes placed below the ground. It would ensure that water drained off the ground very fast, and minimize the possibility of cricket matches being washed out by rain. However, despite all these underground structures, the grass above the ground would stay fully in place. And it had worked perfectly on the night of the final.

Priyamvada recalls her proud feelings on that day:

> Sachin Tendulkar and M.S. Dhoni—they were playing on *my* ground, and the grass had stayed perfectly in place throughout the match. Only a few years ago, when I was looking after my children and my home, I would not have had the confidence or the courage to do this, to work for days on end and launch such an ambitious business venture. At that time, I was out of the work mainstream, and my self-esteem had fallen severely. But then I joined the Tata Second Career Programme (called SCIP), and I discovered myself once again. SCIP gave me back my wings to fly. And how I flew.

Priyamvada is one of the many SCIPPIES, as the alumni of the Tata Second Career Internship Programme, prefer to call themselves. It is a programme that has the potential to unlock the tremendous amount of latent productivity that lies within qualified women who, for myriad reasons, have opted out of the workforce. This could completely change the way women and their employers perceive careers in India.

What is SCIP?

SCIP, launched by the Tata Group in 2008, provides women who have taken a career break with a flexible platform to return to the corporate sector. So many well-qualified, intelligent women put their careers on hold to take care of their young children and families. As the years pass, these women find it increasingly challenging to return to the workplace, despite wanting to do so. SCIP is a very special programme designed to meet these aspirations and to tap into an enormous pool of experience and talent.

What SCIP offers women is a simple, powerful package. It provides attractive internships to women who have taken career breaks on account of personal commitments. By doing this, it eases their return to full-time work, and ensures that they are not lost forever from the productive workforce of the nation.

Satish Pradhan, who heads the human resources function of the Tata Group, is very proud of SCIP.

> When we launched this programme, I was convinced we were doing something that would deliver a breakthrough. When it delivers to its full potential, SCIP will be a big step not only for us in the Tata Group but also for the entire country. We need talented women back in the workforce, but this is unfortunately not happening fast enough.

Roopa Purushothaman, a senior woman manager and one of the authors of the celebrated 2003 Goldman Sachs report that coined the term BRIC nations (for the high-growth countries, Brazil, Russia, India and China), reinforces this sentiment. 'Increasing women's participation in the workforce could be one of the most powerful ways to boost growth, incomes and consumption in India. However, as women become more educated, it appears that they work less and less.'

Rajesh Dahiya now leads the human resources function at one of India's largest and most successful private banks, Axis Bank. He has also worked in the Tata Group for over two decades and played a key role in creating SCIP. He says, 'When qualified women do not return to the workplace, we simply waste top-class talent. And many of these women also end up feeling that they have wasted away their own skills. When they return, we create a win-win situation for all of us. That's why I put SCIP right on top.'

India's leaky pipeline of talent

In the World Economic Forum's 2011 ranking of gender parity in economic participation, India ranks very close to the bottom, and only just above Turkey, Saudi Arabia, Pakistan and Yemen. This gap 'will be detrimental to India's growth', the report points out in a somewhat polite tone. Perhaps the author of this report should have been blunter and used more graphic language that accurately reflects the situation.

Only 22 per cent of India's female graduates enter the workforce. Think about this statistic for a moment. This means that less than a quarter of women graduates, who have studied for at least fifteen years of their lives and acquired full-fledged university degrees, ever put their professional qualifications to any use. This is even lower than the rate of illiterate Indian women who find a job. In comparison, the ratio of female graduates working is more than 40 per cent in South Korea.

The Gender Diversity Benchmark for Asia 2011—published by a Hong Kong–based non-profit organization called Community Business that collects data from several participating companies—highlights that India is consistently the worst performer in the representation of women in the workforce, both in junior and middle-level positions. While the highest proportion of women is employed in these positions in China, the percentage is the lowest in India.

The same report contains several other pieces of data that are shameful in their implications. For instance, in the Indian organizations surveyed, only 52 per cent of the women in junior positions ever make it to middle management. Gender discrimination alone does not account for this colossal loss— the other big reason for it is that many talented women just drop out of the workforce and never return.

The low numbers of women graduates at work in India are also reflected in the boardrooms of companies, where tremendous power is wielded and directions are set. Community Business reports a survey of 100 Indian companies that are on the BSE 100 index, a weighted index of 100 representative stocks in the country. In these companies, out of a total of 1112 directors, only fifty-nine are women. This represents an abysmal woman–power ratio of 5.3 per cent, less than half the ratio in countries such as the USA and the UK.

To sum this up in corporate hierarchy terms: less than a quarter of Indian women graduates enter the workplace, only half of them make it to middle management and only a tiny fraction of them make it to the boardroom. The pipeline is very leaky indeed. It is ironic that, at the same time, Indian companies increasingly struggle to obtain top-class talent. Managers constantly bemoan the lack of adequate skill sets, and consider this their topmost challenge for the future.

Dahiya has regret in his voice when he tells me:

> For organizations today, people quality is the final differentiator. This makes all the difference between mediocre and good performance, between good and great. Overall, as a country, we are constantly going down the slope, on quality of people. No wonder this is happening, because we give little importance to one half of our workforce, to the women who can bring in enormous talent.

Satish Pradhan of the Tata Group gently pats his splendid moustache, and then adds in his uniquely acerbic style:

> We are not positively encouraging of women at work. We do not respect their full identity, which is a beautiful mosaic of professional, creative individual, mother, wife and homemaker. Our companies are inhabited by a dominant male mindset, which indulges at best in tokenism, at worst in complete neglect. That's why our women drop off the radar, and that's such a shame.

India is a country that seeks to be an economic superpower, and therefore needs all the top-class talent it can harness. It is unfortunate that despite all its culture and tradition India cannot provide equal opportunities for women. That's why the Tata Group decided to make a small but meaningful contribution with SCIP in 2008.

The genesis of SCIP

Several years before SCIP began, Ratan Tata had once met a few senior women professionals over dinner. Satish Pradhan recalls the conversations at this event. The challenges and opportunities on the paths of working women were openly discussed. After the initial polite conversation, some real issues bubbled to the surface: the multiple demands on working women, the lack of a work–life balance and the challenges of navigating a predominantly male environment.

A few years later, the Confederation of Indian Industry (CII) constituted a National Committee on Women's Empowerment, headed by Anu Aga, a prominent Indian businesswoman and also an energetic social worker. She had, for many years, successfully led Thermax Limited, a large energy and environment engineering major. More recently, she has also been nominated to the Rajya Sabha by the Government of India.

Pradhan says:

> This committee discussed how we could stem the tide of women leaving the workplace. A relevant topic, and sure enough, a number of good starting points emerged. But to me, some part of this topic felt like flogging a dead horse, because the reasons were well known. And also because thousands of women had already left over a period of several years, and they were out there.

These forums had provoked lingering thoughts on this subject within the corridors of Bombay House. Was there something the Tata Group could do? There was silent recognition of the importance of the matter, since it impacted half the workforce of the country. But there was also determination that the subject should be given serious attention, and not mere lip service.

These thoughts finally came to the fore at a 2007 meeting chaired by R. Gopalakrishnan, executive director, Tata Sons. Held at Hotel President at Cuffe Parade in Mumbai, the meeting was attended by Satish Pradhan, Rajesh Dahiya and the chief human resources officers (CHROs) of several Tata companies. This is a forum that meets periodically to discuss the people agenda in Tata companies and, in internal parlance, is commonly called the CHRO forum. The topic being discussed was large population segments including women. At this meeting, Pradhan and his team argued that the problem should be turned on its head. It was not enough to put in place an environment that retained women professionals, which would certainly help but in a limited manner, since it would be restricted to the respective companies and their employees. It was equally important to bring back to the workforce well-qualified women who had taken a break from their careers, but were still in the prime of their lives. This should cover not only the women who had left the Tata Group but also those who had left their careers in any organization in the country. The impact such an initiative could have on the larger population, and not just the Tata Group, would then be far-reaching. The team felt that this is a role the Tata Group has always tried to play in society, and it should weigh in on a matter as important as this.

Rajesh Dahiya recalls that meeting:

RG [as R. Gopalakrishnan is called by many colleagues] has an excellent sense for picking a big idea. In our minds, we were struggling with our constant search for talent. So, we said, can we come up with an attractive idea that brings back talented women to the workforce? The response from RG was immediate. Yes of course, come up with a good proposal, and we will make it happen.

I have always been gratified to see such instant response by senior directors of the Tata Group, even if the idea being mooted is not for the benefit of the group alone. I thought to myself, this can only happen here. I was excited, I think very excited. Here was an opportunity to make a change for the sake of society.

Some women speak about careers and home

When Rajesh reached his home at Mahalaxmi, Mumbai, that evening, he immediately invited himself to visit other families living in apartments within the same building. He wished to understand for himself why qualified women were not returning to the workplace. Women in many of these homes were his wife's friends, and the men were affluent professionals working in glitzy offices in India's maximum city.

The story was the same in most of these homes. The men

An early Indica drawing

An advertisement for the Second Career Internship Programme

The weavers of Okhamandal

Vhali, the whale shark

A Miss Universe crown created by Tanishq

A bride in the driver's seat in an early advertisement for Tanishq

EKA, the supercomputer

The complicated cabling used for EKA

A character from the Tetley folk

Tata Steel plant

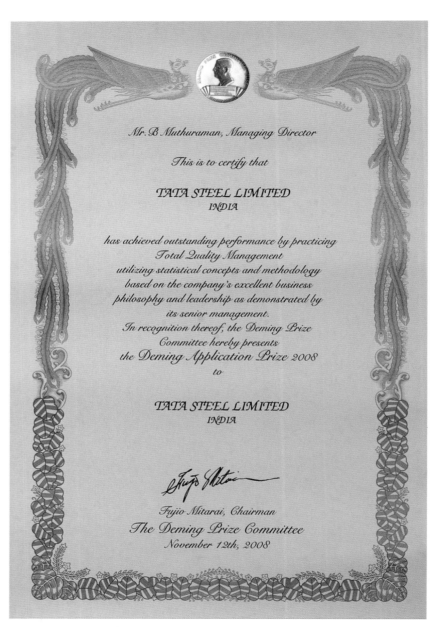

Mr. B Muthuraman, Managing Director

This is to certify that

TATA STEEL LIMITED
INDIA

has achieved outstanding performance by practicing
Total Quality Management
utilizing statistical concepts and methodology
based on the company's excellent business
philosophy and leadership as demonstrated by
its senior management.
In recognition thereof, the Deming Prize
Committee hereby presents
the Deming Application Prize 2008
to

TATA STEEL LIMITED
INDIA

Fujio Mitarai, Chairman
The Deming Prize Committee
November 12th, 2008

The certificate of the Deming Prize, 2008

Tatas acquire stake in Tata Fin arm

Mumbai, July 26: The house of Tatas is said to have have increased their stake in Tata Finance subsidiary Nishkalp to 50 per cent for a consideration of Rs 40 crore. The remaining 50 per cent equity stake of Nishkalp is held by Tata Finance.

Managing director, Tata Finance, Kishore Choukar said, "Tatas have already said they are realigning businesses to maximise synergies. As part of this effort the house of Tatas has picked up stake in Tata Finance."

Refusing to name the group company, Mr Chaukar said it was a Tata Sons company which had acquired the stake.

He however, categorically denied that recent unravelling of unauthorised transactions in Tata Finance could have been reason for the acquisition.

"I do not think the irregularities preempted the stake acquisition. This is normally a long process, and the house of Tatas has increased its stake over the last several weeks," Mr Chaukar said.

Tata Finance is a non-banking finance company with Rs 3,800 crore worth of assets. It has several subsidiary opera-

DAMAGE CONTROL

tions, including Nishkalp (which has ceased to be a subsidiary only from 28 June 2001) which is currently mired in an unauthorised financial transactions' case.

Mr Chaukar said the unauthorised financial transactions via Nishkalp came to light in May 2001.

In a statement, on Wednesday admitted that the board of directors of Tata Finance recently discovered certain unauthorised financial transactions undertaken by "the then management of Tata Finance led by the former managing director Dilip S. Pendse."

"The board of Tata Finance, backed by its promoters, the Tata Group will ensure that Tata Finance meets its financial obligations to lenders and depositors."

The unauthorised transactions include inter alia diversion of funds to Tata Finance's subsidiary Nishkalp Investment and Trading Company and certain other associate companies, whose affairs were also controlled and managed by the then management of Tata Finance, the statement said. *(PTI)*

Crisil downgrades TFL NCDs

The Credit Rating Information Services of India (Crisil) on Tuesday downgraded and removed from rating watch the Rs 260-crore non-convertible debentures, fixed deposit and also the Rs 100-crore commercial paper programmes of Tata Finance Ltd.

Page 2; See also Page 3

Crisil downgrades Tata Fin Rs 260-cr NCDs

Our Banking Bureau
Mumbai, Dec 4

THE Credit Rating Information Services of India (Crisil) on Tuesday downgraded and removed from rating watch the Rs 260-crore non-convertible debenture (NCD), fixed deposit and also the Rs 100-crore commercial paper (CP) programmes of Tata Finance Ltd (TFL).

Further, the Tata group has submitted a letter to the Reserve Bank of India (RBI) giving a broad outline of the restructuring plan, which includes, inter alia, restoring

the capital adequacy ratio of TFL to 12 per cent by December 2002 by infusing Rs 100 crore capital each in December 2001, January-March and December 2002 respectively.

TFL's NCD programme has been downgraded to 'BBB-' from 'A-' indicating moderate safety; the FD programme has been downgraded to 'FA-' from 'FA' indicating adequate safety while the CP programme has been downgraded to 'P3' from 'P2+' indicating adequate safety.

The downgrade in the ratings reflects the deterioration in the credit profile and financial flexibility of TFL following the recognition of large-scale losses in company's books and the consequent knock in the capital position of the company.

TFL's business position has also relatively weakened. However, the ratings in investment grade reflect the significant risk mitigation by way of the publicly affirmed (and demonstrated) liquidity support and proposed recapitalisation plan for TFL by the Tata group, said Crisil.

The revised ratings derive significant comfort from the efforts made by the Tata group to ensure that TFL does not default on it debt obligations.

The support from the Tata group has been demonstrated in the form of liquidity assistance provided to TFL in the form of inter corporate deposits (ICDs) of about Rs 225 crore.

The ratings have been taken off rating watch following the finalisation of the group's plan with regard to TFL's exposure to Nishkalp and associate companies. In the absence of any exceptional strictures so far on the company by the regulators, Crisil expects that the group support available to TFL, would enable it to service its debt obligations in a timely fashion. Crisil would review the ratings of the company, should there be any adverse directives from the regulators to TFL.

The company had reported a large loss of Rs 395.56 crore. The reason for this loss was the substantial provisions for advances and investments made in Nishkalp (Rs 267 crore), exposures to associate companies (Rs 47.2 crore) and non-performing assets and diminu-

tion of value of investments of the order of Rs 72.2 crore. Besides, the core operations of the company have been loss making. The losses have resulted in an extremely weak capital position with a tangible net worth of Rs 53.28 crore (excluding cumulative redeemable preference shares) as against total funds deployed of Rs 3,810 crore as at June 30, 2001.

In view of the diversion of management attention during the past several months towards solving Nishkalp related problems and the exit of some key members of the former management team, the core business of the company has also suffered, resulting in competitors enhancing their relative market position. ◆

Newspaper reports on Tata Finance: (top) in the *Asian Age*, 26 July 2001 and (above) in *Financial Express*, 4 December 2001

Tata Group commits Rs 500 crore to revive Tata Finance

Times News Network

MUMBAI: The Tata Group on Wednesday said it was committed to reviving the beleaguered Tata Finance Ltd by investing up to Rs 500 crore and entering into a joint venture with either an international or domestic partner.

Allaying shareholders fears at the annual general meeting (AGM) in Mumbai, Tata Finance chairman and Tata Sons director Ishaat Hussain said, "The Tata Group reiterates its support to TFL to enable it to meet its obligations to its lenders and fixed deposits."

He said the group has already deposited Rs 100 crore with the finance company, which will result in an increase of the capital adequacy ratio (CAR) to three per cent from the present one per cent.

The company has suffered Rs 396 crore loss for the fiscal ended June 2001. The loss was due to the Rs 315 crore one-time extraordinary provision related to transactions in respect of loans and investments. The company has made a provision of Rs 72 crore towards non-performing assets and diminution in the value of investments, which has resulted in the company reporting a net loss of Rs 80 crore.

He said the company has repaid Rs 123 crore of fixed deposits, which have already been substituted by the funds from the Tata Group. The Group has already invested Rs 146 crore in the capital of TFL & Niskalp. As per the plan, the promoters, along with a strategic partner, will infuse funds—a capital of Rs 100 crore between January and March 2002 and a further capital of Rs 100 crore by December 31, 2002.

Tata Fin to wind up capital market unit

Anand Adhikari
Mumbai, September 4

TATA FINANCE Ltd has informed the Reserve Bank of India that it will bring in another Rs 100 crore by December 2002 to recapitalise the beleaguered nonbanking finance company.

The additional funds would enable the company to achieve the RBI mandated capital adequacy norm of 9 per cent.

The Tata group has already infused Rs 200 crore up to March 2002 in Tata Finance.

Focusing on commercial vehicle financing, TFL is fast exiting from its noncore areas of corporate finance, capital market and credit cards.

The company has discontinued fresh activities of its corporate finance division. "The focus is on recovering amounts already lent. The company is negotiating for the sale of its lease portfolio", TFL officials said.

Tata Finance has also decided not to renew the licenses for merchant banking and underwriting activities. The company's board has recommended winding up the loss making Tata Finance Merchant Bankers Ltd in view of the depressed capital market.

The capital market division reported a loss of Rs 60 lakh.

The company has also downsized its deposit portfolio from Rs 850.96 crore as on July 2001 to Rs 553.14 crore. It has also rationalised its manpower.

Tata scrips take a beating

Our Bureau
MUMBAI, Aug. 8

LEADING Tata group companies took a hit today on the bourses following reports of the withdrawal of the controversial Ferguson report on Tata Finance as well as the resignation of Mr Y.M. Kale, author of the report and partner in the audit firm.

Among the major losers were Tata Finance, Tata Steel, Tata Engineering and Tata Power. Their scrips fell between two and seven per cent over yesterday's closing prices.

The lone gainer in the group was Tata Honeywell.

The fall in the share price of most of the Tata group companies also impacted the stock indices – with the benchmark BSE Sensex going down 59.35

points to close at 2,950.09; and S&P CNX Nifty down 15 points at 953.55.

Other Tata group companies that fared badly today included Indian Hotel, Tata Chemicals, Tata Elxsi, Tata Infomedia, Tata Tea, Tata Telecom, Trent, VSNL and CMC.

Dealers said there was panic selling on the Tata group counters due to the ongoing controversy relating to the AF Ferguson report on the operations of Tata Finance.

Stocks across the board witnessed selling pressure

too, with the old economy shares leading the fall. Sensex heavyweights such as Reliance, HLL, ITC and Infosys ended

lower. Dealers said the rally on the international bourses helped the Sensex to open in the positive zone; but the mood in the market turned bearish soon after.

Pharma stocks such as Glaxo, Cipla and Dr Reddy's Laboratories also witnessed selling pressure.

Larsen & Toubro, one of the few stocks that managed to keep off the red, ended higher due to reports of UTI offloading 10 per cent of its stake in the company. Dealers said speculations that a prominent business group is buying UTI's stake, led to selective buying on the counter.

Newspaper reports on Tata Finance: (clockwise from left) in the *Times of India*, 24 January 2002; in *Hindustan Times*, 4 September 2002; and in *The Hindu Business Line*, 8 August 2002

would say, referring to their wives with pride in their eyes, 'Thanks to Nita (or Hema or Sheetal). She's there for me; she takes care of our home wonderfully well.' They would then explain, 'I am earning quite well now. Her earnings are not required, because I take care of that.' The women would sometimes mention that they were getting bored, but they would mostly accept the husband's words of appreciation. In fact, in such interactions, they seemed quite happy too. Family happiness was paramount.

But longer conversations with them told a different story, and their concerns bubbled up:

'Why will any organization ask me to work for them now? My skills are buried in the past.'

'My husband is a vice-president already. I left my company when I was an assistant manager. I will never catch up now.'

'I used to be a very sharp equity analyst. The day I had a baby, I think my brain went mushy. I was thinking of different things altogether, for weeks and months. I wonder, did my brain get rewired?'

'Of course I would like to get back to work; that will give me a lot of satisfaction. But can I even think of working full-time, with all these multiple demands at home? Maybe NGO-type of part-time work perhaps, sometime in the future.'

Rajesh and his team also spoke to working women who had never taken a break from their careers, many of them in the Taj group of hotels. The Taj group has had a consistent history of women successfully donning key roles, including senior positions in the marketing team, and also as general managers in charge of individual hotels. Their responses once again emphasized what women really desired.

'I pursue my career because it completes who I am. And I have worked without a break because I am fortunate to have a supportive husband.'

Based on these conversations and concerns, the team headed by Satish Pradhan and Rajesh Dahiya established that many women who had taken a break from their careers certainly wished to work again. But there were several questions to answer, and many barriers to cross, before this could happen.

Will I be able to handle a full day's job, with children at home? What will my family think about my returning to work? Will I feel devalued, playing the role of a trainee in a project? My skills are rusty; can I update them after so many years?

A bridge back to work

Pradhan recalls how the team quickly grappled with these issues and zeroed in on some essentials:

> We had to ease the return-to-work cliff into a gradual slope. Here, women and their families could test out the change and gain confidence. Otherwise, the experiment was designed to fail. Therefore, we hit upon the idea of a six-month internship, but an internship that offered a meaningful and engaging assignment. We decided that the correct offering at this stage was not a job for ever, but a bridge back to work.

Pradhan and Dahiya set about building this bridge back to work. They consulted several women working in the Tata Group, to develop the idea. Here is what the initial structure looked like.

The internship would be in a Tata company for an initial period of six months. This is a long enough period to sink one's teeth into a good meaty project. It is also long enough for women to regain confidence in handling work and home simultaneously. To further facilitate confidence building during these initial months, the Tata Group would not insist on fixed working hours. However, the selected women would have to work for a total of 500 working hours during the six months, with flexible day-to-day work timings to be decided in consultation with individual project guides.

The focus would be on experienced and qualified women professionals, since this was the segment where the most amount of productivity was being lost. Hence, the internship would be offered to women with qualifications in management, accountancy, law or engineering, who had at least four years of work experience. This opportunity would be provided to women who had taken a break of one to eight years after the initial years of work. Beyond the internship period of six months, there was no assurance of a full-time job. However, if the Tata companies wished to extend the duration of the assignment or offer a full-time job to the woman concerned, this was perfectly in order. A stipend of Rs 1.5 lakh to Rs 2 lakh would be paid to each participant for the entire period of six months. This would ensure that the overall cost of the programme remained reasonable.

At this stage, the proposal was taken to Gopalakrishnan for his approval and the sanction of budgets. He immediately shot down the stipend, calling it unacceptable. Rajesh thought that Gopalakrishnan was unwilling to provide these budgets due to cost constraints, and feared this would lead to the entire proposal being shelved. So, looking for ways to rescue the programme, he said, 'Sir, in that case, should we think of reducing the stipend?'

Gopalakrishnan's point was, however, exactly the opposite.

'If we are serious about getting top talent back to work, we cannot compromise on pay. We have to pay them what their qualifications and experience justify. Let's double the stipend to Rs 4 lakh for the six-month period. Now that sounds like a reasonable annual pay.'

Many women who have participated in the programme have confirmed later that this was one factor that motivated them to apply.

The team needed to work out a good brand name for the internship. Since it was all about providing 'second careers' to women post a break, these two words were tossed around. 'Second Career Internship Programme' came up as a good branding option, because its acronym, SCIP, had a nice feel to it. It addresses women who have 'skipped' a few years of work, and also evokes the energetic visual imagery of 'skipping' back to work!

Most importantly, various Tata companies had to be taken on board. They had to be briefed about SCIP and its larger purpose. They had to offer meaningful project assignments, and be prepared for flexible timings. Dahiya recalls that there was broad and informal support and acceptance from many companies, who were quite willing to try out the new framework. 'That is part of how the large and extensive Tata network works,' he says. 'We knew many of these senior managers very well over many years, and they are culturally in tune with such socially relevant initiatives. So it was possible for me to pick up the phone and say, "Srinath (or Mukundan or Bhaskar—all CEOs of Tata companies), this is what we want to do, and we require your support." In so many cases, the response was immediate.'

The launch of SCIP

On 8 March 2008, International Women's Day, SCIP was launched in Mumbai. The idea was to first experiment in Mumbai and then take the programme to other cities. The launch announcement and advertisements invited applications from qualified women who had taken a break and who wanted to return to work. Alongside a picture of a young professional woman, the headline read, in big bold letters: 'Resume your career'.

Within a few days, a better line was crafted by the editors of the *Hindustan Times*, which captured the launch in a prominent article. The report was memorably titled 'Say TATA, not goodbye'.

Outdoor hoardings announcing SCIP came up in many parts of Mumbai. Unlike the advertisements for toothpaste or cars or other products that come up in the posh office district of Nariman Point or on the beautiful ocean-facing stretch of Marine Drive, these hoardings were strategically placed in residential areas, or between residential and shopping areas in suburban Mumbai. A large newspaper advertisement also appeared.

It was one of these hoardings that prompted Priyamvada Merchant, the woman engineer who celebrated her personal victory in the Wankhede Stadium, to apply for a SCIP internship. As did Sangeeta Navalkar and Sunita Wazir, both HR professionals, Bharvi Jadhav, a marketing manager, and Sharmila Pandey, a graduate of the Indian Institute of Management (IIM). And thousands of other intelligent, professionally qualified women who had taken breaks in their careers.

Before the week ran out, there were over 7000 inquiries from women in Mumbai. A strong desire that had fallen into voluntary but uneasy slumber appeared to have been suddenly awakened, triggered by the possibilities that SCIP offered. The Tata Group's insights on what would bring women back to work had been absolutely correct!

Pradhan recalls, 'The number of relevant, valid and project-matched applications from women ran into thousands, and far exceeded the projects we could offer. We had to narrow them down. Our brief was clear. We had to select top-class talent. This was not a favour being done to any woman.'

The applications were handled in a sensitive manner. Call-centre associates responding to these women were trained personally by the Tata team, so that they could be as reassuring as possible, while also sticking to the facts. This would help ensure that some women who were still hesitant did not disconnect. Every woman who applied was also sent a personalized copy of *The Creation of Wealth*, which told the story of the Tata Group. This would provide comfort by re-emphasizing both the credentials and the values of the industrial house that was offering these internships.

Finally, SCIP candidates were personally shortlisted and selected by senior executives and HR managers of the Tata Group. Dahiya vividly remembers meeting the first candidate, a graduate of IIM, Kolkata who had more than ten years of work experience before she had taken a break.

'I thought to myself, what a brilliant woman. Why should we ever lose her from the workforce? And I was also constantly thinking of her IIM batchmates, who had already risen to senior positions in the Tata Group.'

That year, out of the thousands who applied, 350 candidates were shortlisted and interviewed telephonically, and 105 women were selected for a panel interview. In the final round, thirty-four women were selected as SCIP interns.

Some SCIPPIES have inspiring stories that demonstrate a burning desire to contribute intellectually and a simultaneous determination to overcome all odds. As a man, I will perhaps never fully understand all the dilemmas, pressures and conflicts which these women have successfully overcome in this quest.

Read on about these remarkable people, and you will see that the Tata SCIP has provided them the platform from which to take a leap, but the strength to do so has come from within these women.

How Priyamvada Merchant SCIPPED into business

My name is Priyamvada and I am a woman of many parts. I love walking in the forests near Mahabaleshwar, I like nature very much; I enjoy writing Marathi poetry. I am confident, but maybe I am a little reserved in my habits.

Today, I manage a successful business called System Rex in Mumbai, which is in the underground drainage business. I am very happy about being able to contribute through this venture. But only a few years ago, it was all quite different and dark. I was struggling with low self-esteem, with two children who needed special care, with no real job, and with many other issues as well. It was a real struggle, those years. I didn't know where I was heading. Until SCIP happened.

I'll start at the beginning. In 1988 I graduated as an electronics and telecom engineer from Aurangabad, and by 1990 I had also completed my postgraduate studies in business management in Mumbai. Thereafter, I worked in Blue Star's medical equipment division. I think I did very well there. Then I got married in 1991 to a boy I loved very much, and the next year we had our first child. We named her Sargam. A beautiful and peaceful name, though what followed what certainly not peaceful for me.

When I went back to office after maternity leave, I just could not work the whole day. I missed my baby, so I informed my boss, and fortunately he understood. I went back home right away on the very first day. A couple of weeks later I resigned from my job. This was a very simple personal decision for me; I could not leave my infant with someone else when I was at work. At that point, I was a mother first and everything else later. For me it was the right thing to do notwithstanding the bright career that I'd be losing out on.

When my daughter was two years old, I decided to go back to work and joined Phillips. An excellent organization, but very soon I faced a problem with my daughter's studies—she was just not performing at school. There was poor feedback from teachers, there were some very tough times at home, but I was determined to get her medically tested. It turned out she had dysgraphia and dyscalculia, both of which are forms of dyslexia. Once again, I gave up my career in Phillips, to ensure that my daughter received all the care and attention she needed. When your child looks you in the eye and silently seeks help, I can tell you, that's all that matters in life.

After extensive research, we used remediation through dance. My daughter learnt Bharatanatyam for several years and excelled in it. She completed her *arangetram* when she was in the eighth standard, and was sent to the USA to represent India. She came back a changed person, her self-esteem high and her spirits even higher. She topped her entire school in two subjects, in the tenth standard ICSE exams. She's a Dorab Tata scholar studying in college today, doing brilliantly. I am so happy with her progress. I am incredibly proud of her today.

But during all these years, I had given up my career. I must confess I was losing confidence in my professional capabilities, even though I had been an outstanding performer at Blue Star so many years ago. At home, the thoughts in my mind were generally dark and brooding. Could I ever stand on my own feet again? Could I cope with a changed office world, which I did not know any more? I felt a great urge to make a difference, to contribute to the external world, but I felt equally helpless about what I should do to make this happen. How could I go back to a very basic job, which I would feel very low about?

But then, who would give me a more meaningful or complex job now?

That's when I first saw the Tata SCIP advertisement. I was excited; I applied immediately. It was like a bright ray of sunshine which had come into my room unexpectedly on a lonely, gloomy day. I had read about the Tata Group; I had visited Tata Motors; I knew they could be trusted. I also thought the Tatas were very professional, but not ruthlessly professional, so they were likely to be flexible to my needs. And they were offering meaningful internships, in keeping with my qualifications and experience. I thank all my stars that I got selected at SCIP. I was so nervous on the day of the interview because I needed this break so badly—for the love of working, and for the money as well.

I was given a wonderful project to work on at Tata Interactive Systems, on identifying CXO proposals for the health-care vertical. It was an interesting, intense and live project, but my manager gave me flexible working hours. I could also make conference calls from home, late in the evening. I loved every moment of the project: we studied products for the health-care industry and 3D simulations that made these products come to life, and methods of marketing them.

But it was much more than the project alone. I met really good people at the company. I spoke with many other SCIPPIES during the initial SCIP induction, which the Tata Group organized for us at the beautiful Tata Management Training Centre in Pune. I saw a professional, safe and good work culture that respected who I was. I began feeling much better. Even as I contributed good work, I felt stronger and lighter. Most importantly, I felt SCIP gave me back my confidence.

I have not looked back ever since. With my confidence back in me, I knew I had to maximize my potential. I knew I was intelligent and skilled; I had to leave my mark somewhere. I decided to establish my own company, called System Rex, in partnership with one of my friends. We had the idea of using corrugated perforated plastic pipes to set up efficient underground drainage at grounds and stadiums. We decided to begin our journey at the Wankhede Stadium in Mumbai, and we went the whole way. We tied up with the architect of the Lord's cricket stadium to understand what they had done; we presented to the Mumbai Cricket Association and obtained their approval; we spoke to Larsen & Toubro who were working on renovating the stadium; we obtained approval from Andy Atkinson of the International Cricket Council. It was a challenging task, but when it worked brilliantly during the World Cup, when the grass stood its ground, we knew we had done it.

There is a huge business scope for underground drainage in stadia, agriculture and several other fields. I want to make my company the best. I know I will make this happen. Life still holds many challenges for me, but SCIP has given me the confidence that I can put my professional skills to work alongside everything I have to do at home.

Anu Unnikrishnan's tale: SCIPPING into 'Jaago Re'

One of the most popular and impactful marketing initiatives seen in India during the past few years has been Tata Tea's 'Jaago Re' campaign. The campaign has beautifully linked the rejuvenating properties of tea to social reawakening, targeting youths and adults alike. While 'Jaago Re' television advertisements have captured popular imagination, their reach and success has also been driven in equal measure by online campaigns, on all digital media.

Working hard on creating and propagating these digital marketing campaigns at Tata Global Beverages (the company that markets Tata Tea) is a peppy, young woman named Anu

Unnikrishnan. Anu speaks with a happy lilt in her voice, as she recalls her first job after college, at the *Times of India*. Joining them in 2001, she handled a supplement called *ASCENT* that featured articles about the workplace and had a classified section for job advertisements as well. With professional qualifications in English literature and marketing management, this seemed like an apt choice.

In 2004, Anu married Sandeep Kaimal, who was based in Bangalore. She worked for a brief period with the *Princeton Review*, which offers training programmes for competitive examinations, and thereafter with the corporate sales team of Radio Mirchi, a popular FM radio station. In 2006, her son was born, and she proceeded to go on a maternity break.

'Being a mother was such a happy moment, but that was also such a chaotic period,' Anu recalls. 'My husband was transferred to Chennai around the same time, so I moved there with him. I had to leave my job. My career had always been part of my identity, and here I was, suddenly moving from one identity to another. I was very frightened.'

Anu says her husband was and continues to be very supportive of her career, but for several years circumstances did not permit her to get back to full-time work. Looking after the child was a complete job by itself. Thereafter, her husband moved places a couple of times, and in 2008, the family relocated to the UK. Eventually, they returned to India. But the demands of motherhood and these constant movements meant that she could never work for substantial hours at a stretch. She did take up some part-time assignments but they did not fulfil her need for intellectual challenges or economic independence.

Anu explains why:

> We were raised no different from boys in our home. I was fortunate to belong to a well-educated family: my mother

works in Kendriya Vidyalaya [India's premier chain of schools, managed by the Central government]. Discussions at home were always about careers and education, rarely about marriage or babies. I grew up with the idea of economic independence and financial security for women. Marriage was important, being a mother was very fulfilling, but so was the idea of a job.

When Anu and her husband returned to India, she applied for jobs and interviewed with a few companies. But they rejected her candidature, questioning her long sabbatical from work.

These companies probably thought that if I had taken such a long career break, I was not serious about work. They did not look at the break favourably at all. One of them, a company in the information technology space, in fact told me—you are a big HR risk. Those words were so upsetting. They took no effort at all to understand how skilled I was, and under what personal circumstances I had taken a long break from work. I sat down one day and I felt the corporate world is so unfair to women and to me.

It was around this time that Anu saw the SCIP advertisement and at first thought it was too good to be true, with the flexible timings and attractive remuneration that was on offer. She applied and was selected.

SCIP was such a liberating experience. To begin with, I met up with around thirty other women at the SCIP induction in Tata Management Training Centre, Pune. It was reassuring to hear their stories, to know that there was such a large talent pool seeking exactly what I was searching for. We were in similar boats, and we were determined.

Anu's internship was with Tata Global Beverages, where she has continued to work for several years thereafter. She was assigned to the 'Jaago Re' campaign, with clearly defined deliverables of overhauling the website and creating a 'Jaago Re' community.

> It was a very professional, flexible and relaxed experience. I think I have added a lot of value, but it is also very nice that office out here feels almost like home. Tata Global Beverages have continued to employ me, to keep the 'Jaago Re' digital thread alive. They have been sensitive to my needs; I get the required time with my child. I have responded with my work as splendidly as I can.

Anu says SCIP has put her back in touch with her profession, and provided her an opportunity like no other. She points out that the internship helped update her knowledge, and today she is capable of cutting-edge work in digital marketing. Most importantly, she says, SCIP gave her confidence in herself, which was badly lacking when several companies refused to recruit her. Like the 'Jaago Re' campaign that exhorts people to reawaken their civic sensibilities, SCIP reawakened and rejuvenated her professional spirit.

Each SCIP story is different

In both these cases, SCIP splendidly met its objective—providing women a bridge back to work. The six-month internship helped to attract them back to work, update their skills and, most of all, give them confidence that they could handle the requirements of office work alongside the demands of home. While Priyamvada went ahead to establish her own business, Anu has stayed on to work with the Tata Group. In one case, the Tata Group has directly benefited. But in both cases, there are two clear winners: the women and society.

The stories of many other SCIP women follow different paths, but some threads are common. For Sunita Wazir, an alumna of the very first SCIP batch, getting back to work after devoting nearly two years to her toddlers meant a series of steep challenges. She says SCIP was tailor-made for her in addressing these issues, and has facilitated both her professional and personal growth. Ruma Rao has gone ahead to work full-time with the Tata Group, and interestingly manages the SCIP programme today in the group's central human resources department. For her, SCIP reignited her desire to work, and showed her that a comeback was possible.

Not all SCIPPIES crossed the bridge successfully, though. A few internships were abandoned midway, because the interns found the pressures too hot to handle. Some internships failed due to poor organization by specific Tata companies or indifferent project guides. Some internships were plain disappointing, because of poor content. Some SCIPPIES went back to part-time or freelance work even though they were given appropriate roles, thereby choosing not to return to the workplace.

Despite these occasional failures and dropouts, there is overall consensus among participants that the SCIP story is a happy one. This quote from SCIPPY Harini Iyer captures what many participants have felt: 'SCIP provides just the right platform to resume one's career after a break, by gently easing us back to the demands of balancing work with family.'

The makings of a big idea

In the first four years since its launch, 104 women have interned in SCIP. For most of these women, SCIP has rewritten the story of their lives, and brought excellent talent back to the workforce. Clearly, it is a big idea that has worked.

SCIP is also a unique idea. There are many reputed

corporations worldwide, for instance Procter & Gamble, that have devised flexible policies to nurture the female employee throughout her career cycle in the company—from recruitment to training to promotion to retention. Many of these policies are worthy of emulation. SCIP, however, was the first structured programme that went beyond narrow corporate boundaries and made a real effort to bring back into our companies women who had taken breaks and left the workforce.

This is characteristic of the Tata Group. When it recognizes the social impact of a big idea, it casts the net far and wide.

Pradhan is emphatic when he says, 'Only the Tata Group could have created SCIP. I can't think of any other corporate that would invest several crore rupees in an idea like this, year after year. The business benefit to the Tata Group is limited, at least in the short term. And we must understand that this is a very long drawn-out process; it will take several years to build a sustainable model.'

He adds, 'This is one of the most important ideas of our generation. Most women who drop out of the workforce never return, and women are half our population. We now have proof of concept that SCIP can engineer second careers for them. The challenge ahead of us is to scale up the programme, to create real impact.'

When will SCIP create real impact?

Four years after the launch, the idea of SCIP continues to remain much larger than the impact it has created. The number of internships over this period is a small and insufficient drop in a vast ocean. Real impact is still far away. It can be created when the Tata Group offers a minimum of 1000 SCIP internships every year. That will create critical mass and will encourage hundreds of large Indian companies to launch similar programmes of their own. Such rapid scaling up is the real challenge that SCIP faces today.

Radhakrishnan Nair, who now heads talent acquisition for the Tata Group and also oversees the SCIP programme, has made a good start by moving to a continuous harvesting model. Applications to SCIP are no longer restricted to once a year. Women can apply for internships any time during the year through a customized website, and projects for these internships are also provided by Tata companies as and when they arise. This move has the potential of multiplying the number of applications manyfold. But Nair wants to push a much faster pace, to reach the 1000 per year milestone.

'We have to heighten awareness of this programme among all Tata companies. The purpose has to be widely known and celebrated. And we also have to make our managers comfortable with the concept of flexi-time working. Only then will many more internship assignments be forthcoming.'

Ruma Rao, who heads SCIP in Nair's team, adds two important points:

> We also need strong support from chief executive officers of the Tata Group. SCIP has to be on the people agenda of each Tata leader. Most important, we need the support of men at various levels, within our companies. Sometimes, they feel that the SCIP provides unfair advantage to the women interns by giving them flexi-time options, whereas no such options are available to men working full-time. But we should all understand the multiple challenges that working women face, particularly when they are just getting back to work.

Pradhan agrees: 'This is too valuable an idea to permit a fade-out. SCIP creates second careers for women, and it also enables us as a working community to respect the needs of women.'

Respect for women

While SCIP has been a wonderful initiative by the Tata Group, it can play only a small role in plugging the leaky pipeline of talent. Our workforce will be severely depleted, and the problem of Indian women dropping out of the workforce like lemmings from a cliff will continue, until there is genuine respect for their capabilities, circumstances and needs.

In conclusion, I hope Nair's words resonate within us all:

> Women in our society are naturally disrespected. We expect them to work hard at home, even if they work hard in offices. We should ask ourselves: How often do I help my wife run the household? How often do I wash my own plates? How often do I look after the children in a meaningful way? Do we take women's needs for granted, most of the time if not always? These attitudes have to genuinely change, only then will we see many more women at work, and also many more open mindsets in our offices. Women help corporates become mature; their feminine skills play an important role in fostering a happy and balanced organization. That's why it is doubly important for SCIP to get women back to work.

EKA: Birth of an Indian Supercomputer

'The only way of discovering the limits of the possible is to venture a little way past them into the impossible.'

—Arthur C. Clarke

'Supercomputing is part of the corporate arsenal to beat rivals by staying one step ahead on the innovation curve. It provides the power to design products and analyse data in ways once unimaginable.'

—*The Secret Weapon*, a report by the US Council on Competitiveness, 2008

The magic of supercomputers

A tall, sleek computer called Deep Blue, created by IBM, defeated the world chess champion Gary Kasparov in 1997. It was the first time that a computer had defeated the world's number one ranked player in tournament conditions. Deep Blue was so fast that it was capable of evaluating 200 million positions on the chess board—in a single second. Several years later, a supercomputer called Watson, again an IBM creation, is challenging human beings at board games. This time, it is taking on champions at *Jeopardy!*, a very popular television game show in the USA. Watson is designed to further the science of natural language processing. It can process about one million books in a single second; its brain is filled with extraordinary knowledge including literary works, articles and databases of all sorts. It is mounted on ten refrigerator-sized racks and has been called Deep Blue's grandchild. In 2011, a Japanese supercomputer called Kei dethroned American and Chinese machines to become the world's fastest supercomputer. 'Kei' is the Japanese Kanji letter for ten quadrillion (that is, one followed by sixteen zeroes), and this computer is capable of mindboggling speed. It can make 8.2 quadrillion calculations per second!

Apart from winning chess and *Jeopardy!* games with astonishing ease, supercomputers are capable of solving complex problems very fast. They help scientists in important areas such as accurate weather forecasting, aerodynamic research, nuclear test simulation, car design and life-saving drugs. These involve very large and complex computations, which makes a really high-speed supercomputer essential. Until 2007, India was not represented in this elite set of countries with the most powerful supercomputers. For a country that is considered an economic engine of the world, this was an unpardonable omission. Enter EKA, the supercomputer built by the Tata Group.

This is the story of how EKA was born—a story whose end is yet to be written.

Tatas and supercomputers

S. Ramadorai, who turned Tata Consultancy Services (TCS) into a global information technology powerhouse and is its vice-chairman today, talks about the long Tata association with supercomputers: 'The Tatas have had a history in this field. Way back in the 1980s, we had an association with Elxsi, who were working on large mainframe computers. We built some large machines, and TCS bought one of them. We used it primarily for research and development. That company, however, could not sustain.'

He goes on to say that supercomputers in India were being actively pursued by very select organizations, the most prominent being the Department of Atomic Energy and the Bhabha Atomic Research Centre (BARC). PARAM, India's first supercomputer, created in 1991, never made it to the top echelons of this field. Neglecting supercomputers is a colossal error, because critical national sectors like defence and nuclear energy require these powerful machines for their development.

Circa 2000, TCS began recruiting scientists who were passionate about supercomputing and other related areas such as VLSI (very large-scale integration) design. One such scientist was Dr Sunil Sherlekar, a prominent research scholar with a doctoral degree from IIT Bombay. He had developed a keen interest in scientific parallel computing. This technical term simply means that individual computers would hold each other's hands and work together on a single problem. Sherlekar was in contact with his classmate, Dr Narendra Karmarkar, the noted Indian mathematician who developed Karmarkar's algorithm, a cornerstone in the field of linear programming. Discussions between the two friends turned to the area of supercomputing and soon, with excitement and enthusiasm, Sherlekar had made his way to Ramadorai's corner office.

'We would like to build a supercomputer,' he told Ramadorai. 'Will the Tatas support this?'

By no stretch of the imagination was this a routine request. Building such a machine is a very challenging technical and financial proposition. It was an ambitious goal. Yet Ramadorai immediately saw the great impact such a project could have, for the country and for the Tata Group. He says, 'I wrote out a note to Ratan Tata, suggesting that this is an idea we should look at. Mr Tata met Sherlekar and Karmarkar, listened to their proposal and responded encouragingly.'

Sherlekar recalls five meetings with Ratan Tata, where the supercomputer concept and proposal were discussed. Ratan Tata was excited, but he insisted that a detailed business plan be written out. The plan would establish whether the proposal made economic sense. Sherlekar recalls Ratan Tata telling him, 'It is not my money, so write a business plan.' So they wrote a business plan, assisted by some members from the Tata Strategic Management Group. That plan was the blueprint for EKA.

The business plan envisaged a commercial launch of the Tata supercomputer by November 2007. This would be a huge computer with a capacity of 1 petaflop (which is equal to 1000 teraflops)—the equivalent of around 20,000 ordinary computers put together. But Ramadorai adds a note of caution: 'That comparison is totally inadequate. It is like comparing an aeroplane with 20,000 bicycles.' Such a supercomputer would not only be the fastest in the world, it would also catapult India into a seat that had so far been occupied by countries such as the USA and Japan. The world of supercomputers would never be the same again.

The plan called for a total investment of US$130 million by the Tatas. It also included a revenue plan of US$240 million that would be generated by the supercomputer through three streams: sales or new installations, renting capability and annual maintenance contracts. Based on these projections, it could be concluded that a supercomputer would not only enhance national pride, it would also be profitable. The plan argued that this was the right time to enter the industry. Critical to the success of the plan was the mechanism that would interconnect all the individual processors of the computer, which is really the backbone of a supercomputer.

In March 2006, Sherlekar and Karmarkar presented the plan to the board of directors of Tata Sons. No one in India had ever envisaged building this powerful computer. The complexities of creating such a splendid beast were unknown. Globally, such computers were generally built by the government or its agencies, but in this case there was no government interaction. If it was approved, it would be a completely Tata-funded project.

The Tatas decide to support EKA

At that momentous meeting, after a detailed discussion, the directors of the apex board of the Tata Group decided to support and drive the EKA project. This was a bold decision, because, borrowing a phrase from the famous television series *Star Trek*, it was like going 'where no man had gone before'.

Recalling this decision, Sherlekar says, 'The Tatas announced their support even before a formal contract was signed, and they did it with very good spirit. The scientific community in India will always remember this decision with pride.'

Raju Bhinge, CEO of Tata Strategic Management Group that had helped Sherlekar and Karmarkar put the plan together, adds, 'We also decided that we would manage the project like any venture capitalist. We defined intermediate milestones, and the investments required for each of these. So, to finally reach 1000 teraflops, we said we should first make a 1 teraflops machine, then 100 teraflops, and after that 400 teraflops.'

A new company, Computational Research Laboratories (CRL), was established to implement this project. Pune, the largest city in the Western Ghats, was chosen as the location. This lovely city has a growing information technology industry, and is also home to the Centre for Development of Advanced Computing (C-DAC). Ramadorai was appointed chairman of the new company. Research engineers were recruited, and a brilliant team soon began working. There was a lot of energy and excitement all around, because this was not just another project.

A founder quits the EKA project

A prototype of a 10-teraflop computer was first created. This was of course much smaller than the ultimate objective, which was 1000 teraflops. But it was an essential step in the journey, to get comfortable with the engineering and test reliability. Meanwhile, various interconnect mechanisms were also being considered, some new and untested, others well known to the supercomputer community.

In July 2007, there was an unexpected development, with the potential to derail the project. Karmarkar, one of the key people and a founder member, decided to quit the project. He had developed differences with the Tata Group regarding how the project should progress, and despite personal efforts by Ratan Tata, these could not be resolved. At a meeting held in the Lake House that adjoins the Tata Motors factory in Pune, a decision was taken to part ways.

Karmarkar was quoted in the *Economic Times*, India's leading business newspaper, as saying he had developed irreconcilable differences over the basic objectives behind the project. He went on to say, 'Apart from generating great returns for the investors, I also had a larger vision to use this technology to drive scientific development both within the country and the rest of the world.'

A departure such as this could have paralysed the project, since Karmarkar's technical knowledge was very important. It is once again to the credit of the Tatas that they decided to persist and go ahead. Ramadorai spoke to Sherlekar, who immediately confirmed his team's and his own confidence in taking the project forward. He called the project not merely exciting, but the grand prospect of a lifetime. He had concerns on various fronts, but he had faith in his team's capability to pull through. They saw no reason to give up the opportunity to create the country's first supercomputer, a distinction that would live in history forever.

Sherlekar recalls with happiness an accidental meeting with Ratan Tata during those anxious days.

> I was attending an Annual General Managers' Meeting of the Tata Group and after the meeting got over there was an excellent lunch at the Taj Residency Hotel. Ratan Tata was there; he had addressed all of us. Now, he was in the dining area, speaking informally to managers over lunch. I was trying my best to avoid him, perhaps because my friend had left the EKA project recently. Suddenly, I felt a tug at my elbow, and I turned around. It was Ratan Tata. He said, 'You know, I am sorry we could not reach an agreement with Karmarkar. But you have a good team. I know you can take it forward.'
>
> It was a wonderful gesture, and it touched me. There was no need really for the chairman of the country's largest industrial group to come up to me and say sorry for a professional disagreement with a colleague.

We must run now

Ramadorai, Sherlekar and a few others now went into a huddle on the way forward for EKA after Karmarkar's sudden departure. Two decisions were quickly taken and ratified by the board of CRL. First, the supercomputer would certainly be built. It was too important a project to be dependent on one individual. In any case, Sherlekar and his team were very confident. It was also established that the machine could be built without violating any intellectual property rights.

Ramadorai recalls mulling over this decision, and consulting Ratan Tata as well. 'Finally, I decided that we had to proceed. We had to show the world that we had come of age in high-performance computing.'

Second, the objective of the project was altered. Rather than creating a 1-petaflop (1000 teraflops) supercomputer, the team would concentrate their energies on creating a 100-teraflop machine by the original target date of 2007. Such a supercomputer may not be the fastest in the world, but it stood a good chance of making it into the top ten. For India and the Tata Group, this would be a big breakthrough. The more powerful 1-petaflop supercomputer could follow after some time.

The investment in a 100-teraflop machine, around US$20 million, was large, but it was more manageable than the US$130 million allocated to building the 1-petaflop machine. The challenge was to create this supercomputer by October 2007, to meet the next deadline for the global supercomputer rankings, which were announced in November, the month when the International Conference for High Performance Computing, Networking, Storage and Analysis (ICHPCNSA) would be held at Reno, Nevada that year. Sherlekar explains:

> If we missed that date, we would have had to wait until June of the next year. Because the field of supercomputers moves so rapidly, many other faster machines are born every month. With a delay, our chances of making it to the top ten would have come down dramatically, and one of our important

goals would be lost. That made us very determined to deliver by October.

Seetha Rama Krishna was a young engineer from Andhra Pradesh who was part of Sherlekar's team. He was given charge of the complex engineering that went into building the hardware of a supercomputer. Ramadorai's words still ring in Seetha's mind: 'We must be in the top ten in the world. And we must run now.'

EKA, one of a kind

Many parents decide on a name for their child well before it is born; they even have male and female options worked out. Ramadorai performed this happy parental duty for the Tata supercomputer, though he did not have to deal with the added complexity of human gender. The choice of name reveals the deep desire that drove the project. IBM has generally named its supercomputers after corporate symbols. Deep Blue, which defeated the chess champion Kasparov, was so named because IBM is referred to as the Big Blue. Watson, the champion *Jeopardy!* playing machine, was named after the first president of the company, Thomas J. Watson. In similar vein, Ramadorai could have called the machine Super-Tata or even Jeh, the name used for J.R.D. Tata by his friends.

Instead, he named it EKA, which means 'one' in Sanskrit. The choice of a Sanskrit word, unconscious though it may have been, illustrates the national pride inherent in this project. Sanskrit lies at the root of Indian culture and is the language in which most ancient Hindu texts were created. The specific word 'eka' evokes the pioneering desire to be first. In fact, it implies 'one of a kind', and is symbolic of the many firsts that this supercomputer would eventually achieve.

Sherlekar, Seetha and other members of the team were working furiously, round the clock, to create EKA. The directors of CRL had communicated their decision to go ahead with the project on 3 September. There were less than seven weeks to meet the October deadline.

There were many large technical challenges to be mastered. A supercomputer requires several kilometres of cables that connect individual processors. Such complex cabling had never been attempted in India before. Seetha and his team decided to use optical cables, which use pulses of light to transmit data. The ability of the cables to perform had just been proven at Intel Laboratories, but the sheer length of cable needed wasn't available from a single vendor.

'That's why we had to use different colours of cables,' says Seetha, 'because each company sent us a different colour. So when you visit EKA you will see cabling in orange and yellow and blue. Mr Ramadorai spoke to Intel, which helped us get these cables fast.'

Then, there was the interconnect technology that needed to be put in place to link these cables. The team decided to use the innovative Infiniband technology, which can deliver high transmission rates. Interconnect equipment was obtained from Mellanox, an Israeli company headquartered both in Yokneam, Israel and in California, USA. Seetha knew the chief technology officer of Mellanox, and his technical expertise helped to develop the interconnect solution for EKA.

Finally, there was the hot challenge of cooling EKA. When a supercomputer works, it consumes huge amounts of electricity and generates equally large quantities of heat, which can prove fatal to the machine, so cooling systems have always been the bugbears of supercomputers. The team developing EKA came up with a very innovative solution. Normally, supercomputers comprise individual processors arranged in neat rows, with the cooling circulating from the floor. The EKA team developed a circular architecture, where the supercomputer looks virtually like a circle. Cooling is achieved by blowing cold air in from the periphery as hot air is then quickly extracted from the top.

Sherlekar describes this cooling system with the pride of a successful innovator: 'We went circular. The outer circle is cold, the inner circle is hot. In a single stroke, this gave us several advantages. Fluid resistance came down. There was no mixing of hot and cold aisles. And we could place the interconnect switch right at the centre!'

Using these technologies, EKA was carefully constructed from scratch. Off-the-shelf servers from Hewlett Packard were used for the individual processors. The team went without sleep for days together, and dealt with unseasonal rainfall. On one particular day, the rainfall was so heavy that the location, which was under construction, was completely submerged. But matters were quickly brought under control. To ensure speedy progress, technological collaboration was obtained from Emerson, Voltas and Tata Consulting Engineers.

Finally, after six weeks of work, EKA was ready on 20 October. But once again, a major problem suddenly reared its head and threatened the very objective of the project.

Beer, cigarettes and supercomputers

If EKA had to be ranked among the top ten supercomputers in the world, crossing a speed of 100 teraflops was essential. This speed is calculated based on how fast the computer can complete a specific task. For supercomputers, the accepted benchmark is LINPACK, a system of complicated linear mathematical equations that have to be solved. When EKA was first given this task on 20 October, everyone held their breath. Then, there was disappointment. EKA had clocked in only 97 teraflops, well short of 100. This happened again, and again. Indians may well compare this to the iconic cricketer Sachin Tendulkar, who reached the 90s several times, but repeatedly fell short of his hundredth international century.

Seetha recalls:

> We just could not understand the reason for this. Everything had been done, but we were not reaching the 100 mark. We racked our brains, and camped next to the supercomputer all day, hoping it would help! Then I remembered some Russian scientists whom I knew well, and who would know exactly what to do in this situation. I traced them down. I found them on the other side of the world, in Mexico. They were working with Intel. There is something most Russian scientists have in common. They generally love Charminar cigarettes and Kingfisher beer. I knew this very well, so I called them and said, 'Help me solve this problem, and I will send you an entire crate of Kingfisher beer!' I could practically see their eyes light up at the other end of the telephone.

This generous offer of Indian beer appears to have helped immediately. The Russian scientists, after obtaining permission from Intel, helped Seetha with his problem. It was resolved just hours before the deadline.

On 31 October, at 8.30 p.m., EKA went well past the century mark and clocked in 118 teraflops. There was a loud round of applause which appeared never to stop, and then there was a deep, respectful silence. Seetha went back to his office to email the data to Jack Donggara of the committee that evaluates the top 500 supercomputers to decide on the global rankings. When he returned to the supercomputer centre, he found everyone fast asleep. 'But they were smiling, all of them,' he says. 'It was the sleep of satisfaction.'

On top of the world

The top 500 supercomputer rankings were to be announced at the ICHPCNSA on 6 November 2007. Ramadorai had set the team a target: to be in the top ten. Would EKA make it, and create history for India and the Tatas? These were nail-biting moments for Sherlekar, Seetha and the team. When the rankings were declared, EKA stood fourth. The team had created the fourth fastest supercomputer in the world, beating machines from every other continent.

'I could not believe it!' Seetha says. 'We were fourth in the world! Yes, we were! India and the Tatas stood fourth, on our very first attempt!'

Sherlekar was sleeping in his mother's home in Pune when he received Seetha's call, well past midnight, informing him of this heady news. He listened, smiled and sent Ramadorai a text message on his mobile. He received an immediate response: 'Congratulations! India must announce this to the world!' Ramadorai says this landmark achievement gave him the same fulfilment as he had felt one late night in 1974, when the first Burroughs mainframe computer had been switched on successfully on the tenth floor of the Air India building in Mumbai. This was the office of TCS, at that time a fledgling company. Radiating satisfaction, Ramadorai unveiled EKA's landmark achievement to the world at a Mumbai press conference. Media reports were glowing in their tribute.

The *Economic Times* said: 'The supercomputer named EKA, the first supercomputer to have been developed totally by a corporation without any government help, now shares the rarefied heights of supercomputing with two American and one German supercomputer.'

IEEE Spectrum, a well-regarded magazine published by the Institute of Electrical and Electronics Engineers, said that the 'global computing community were surprised' when EKA made it to the coveted fourth rank. Such ranks are normally the domain of national laboratories in the richest countries, it added.

EKA's performance reverberated throughout the supercomputing industry. US laboratories immediately saw this as a threat to their dominance of high-performance computing. They demanded higher resources to develop a new generation of supercomputers. When Tata scientists visited some of these laboratories later, they were received with newfound respect. There are also some unconfirmed reports that the Chinese authorities were furious when they heard of EKA. They called Mellanox Technologies, which had given EKA the Infiniband technology, and asked that they create a similar supercomputer for China. At that time, China had no significant presence in supercomputers. Today, the position is quite different—they have begun dominating this area. One reason for such global shock and surprise was that the Tata team had carefully camouflaged the development of EKA as the creation of a large in-house computer facility for computing and the requirements of management information systems (MIS) of the Tata Group. 'We did not want problems with some foreign governments putting a brake on supplies of technology,' says Seetha. 'That is why we chose to do this.'

EKA and India's moon vehicle

Once the initial euphoria of being fourth fastest in the world had calmed down, the scientists who made EKA got down to a different kind of work. They had to show that a supercomputer was not merely a symbol of national pride; it could also be put to good and viable use in India.

One of the first big contributions from EKA came during another project of national pride, Chandrayaan. This was India's moon vehicle, the country's first unmanned lunar probe. It is credited with the discovery of the widespread presence of water molecules in the moon's soil. EKA partnered with the Indian Space Research Organization (ISRO) on some important aspects of the Chandrayaan launch. A very challenging aspect in such an effort is predicting weather at the time of the launch. Anything less than perfect weather prediction can ruin an expensive and prestigious space effort. EKA was pressed into the effort, crunching massive amounts of data rapidly. A dedicated leased line from SHAR, the launch centre at Sriharikota, to the EKA centre in Pune was used.

Sherlekar says, 'This was a big test for us. EKA worked hard, and its weather predictions turned out to be absolutely perfect. Its calculations had predicted a precise window of time when rains would stop at Sriharikota, the launch site. And rains stopped exactly at that time, creating the perfect weather for the launch of Chandrayaan!'

The ex-chairman of ISRO, G. Madhavan Nair, publicly expressed appreciation for the brilliant work done by EKA and the team at CRL, where the supercomputer is housed. His letter was read out aloud by EKA's scientists to Ramadorai:

> I would like to state that the weather forecasting made by our modelers at SHAR during the PSLV-C11 launch using high-performance clusters at CRL was an excellent piece of work and helped ISRO teams to run the models four times a day. The CRL team provided excellent support in porting MM5 and WRF models, and in executing these models quite efficiently and fast. The computational time for six-hour predictions at the CRL facility took less than ten minutes for the WRF model, as against three hours in the 16-node cluster

at ISRO. Due to the computing efficiency, the ISRO team could run six-hour predictions on the day of the launch to confirm reduced rainfall activity during launch time. Besides, the Vikram Sarabhai Centre team also extensively used the CRL facility for computational fluid dynamics simulations, and derived great benefit. I appreciate the cooperation, support and services provided by the CRL team to ISRO during the PSLV-C11/Chandrayaan 1 launches. I congratulate all the team members for the excellent contribution and the facility in ready state-of-the-art.

Making a mark in other areas

EKA quickly began making a mark in many other areas that required data-intensive computing, including the automotive industry, animation movies and aerospace design.

Working closely with another Tata company, Tata Elxsi Limited, the supercomputer helped create India's first fully animated, full-length, three-dimensional (3D) feature film, *Roadside Romeo*. Romeo, the roadside dog who is the hero of this celluloid love story, and Laila, his canine girlfriend, were created and animated using the extraordinary power of EKA. The time to render each animated frame was reduced by at least 40 per cent, and the time required to release this film was reduced by at least five months. EKA was also used to help aerospace companies such as Boeing and Piaggio Aero accelerate product development life cycles and reduce costs. Supercomputers have become essential to developing new aircraft. If seventy-seven prototypes were used to develop an aircraft wing back in 1980, the use of powerful supercomputers now enables the same work to be done by using only seven prototypes, which implies one-tenth the effort. Doug Ball of the Boeing Corporation says, 'Our work with supercomputers allows us to get a better product out of the door faster, which makes us more competitive.' In the exciting field of motor racing, EKA forged a partnership with India's first Formula 1 team, Force India. The supercomputer's capabilities would be used to develop the next generation race cars for this team, as well as improve the aerodynamic efficiency of the current racing models. The sheer computing power of EKA would sharply reduce design cycle times for improvements, thus giving Force India drivers their best chance of a strong result.

It must be mentioned that the Force India team is owned by Dr Vijay Mallya, the Indian business tycoon who also makes Kingfisher beer. Since the offer of Kingfisher beer to Russian scientists had helped resolve an important issue in the initial development of EKA, readers will note that the wheel had now come full circle.

There were many other interesting areas in which EKA was used. Dr Vipin Chaudhury, a renowned authority on supercomputing, who has now succeeded Sherlekar as director of CRL, speaks about all these applications with great passion and conviction.

'EKA has been used to develop new nanofluids, in design work and to improve the external aerodynamics of passenger cars. It has reduced design time hugely, reduced error rates from 30 per cent to 3 per cent in aircraft simulations, and reduced turnaround times for specific jobs by 50 per cent. There are multiple benefits here: accuracy, throughput and cost. That's why supercomputers like EKA will redefine the possible.'

But Chaudhury also points out the challenge of generating consistent business. Most Indian organizations, he says, are yet to wake up to all the possibilities of supercomputing, and the idea is still ahead of its time.

The Tatas had put India firmly on the world supercomputing map. Before the development of this landmark machine, only two nations, USA and Japan, had supercomputers with the capability of 100 teraflops or more. Thanks to the vision and courage displayed by the Tata Group, India had entered this elite league.

Many decades ago, Tata leaders had set up pioneering institutions such as the Indian Institute of Science, the Tata Institute of Fundamental Research, the Tata Memorial Hospital and the National Centre for the Performing Arts. They had established capabilities for manufacturing steel and generating hydroelectric power in India. The development of EKA certainly belonged in that class of achievement. The Tata Group felt the need for powerful supercomputing facilities to service the requirements of industry, including automobiles, software, drug design and oil and gas exploration. The idea that supercomputing could be a differentiator for the nation's economy also appeared to be a key motivator. Since supercomputing was a neglected area, both in terms of investment and applications, the Tatas had decided to enter this field.

EKA was thus a development of national significance and not merely a business effort. However, this pioneering thrust may soon be lost.

The world moves on

In 2007, EKA was ranked the fourth fastest supercomputer in the world. By 2009, it had slipped to twenty-first in the global rankings. By 2011, it had slipped further to eighty-fifth. It may soon fall out of the top 100 altogether.

The reason for this plunge in EKA's rankings is that, over the past few years, other countries and corporations have invested huge amounts in developing supercomputers which are far more powerful. At the time of writing, there are more than ten supercomputers in the world which have a computing power above 1 petaflop. There were none in 2007. One must note the spectacular progress made by China, which did not have a single supercomputer in the top ten in the year of EKA's birth. However, recognizing the strategic national importance of supercomputers to a country's development, including essential applications in internal security and defence, China went into overdrive. Today, there are two Chinese supercomputers in the top five in the world, and four in the top twenty.

What has happened to the original goal set out by the Tatas: the creation of a 1-petaflop supercomputer after testing the success of EKA's 100 teraflops? There has been occasional talk of developing an EKA Plus, or substantially bettering EKA's performance and architecture. However, the 1-petaflop machine is not yet in sight.

It is likely that hard business realities and the significant costs involved have stalled these grand plans. Generating for a large supercomputer adequate commercial business to fully compensate these large costs may yet be several years away. Industrial applications in India continue to lag behind, though supercomputing capability may well be an essential ingredient in the development of breakthrough products. In the national interest, our country must invest confidently to make the next breakthrough in supercomputing possible. Similar to nuclear or space capability, a supercomputer is a symbol of national pride, and also essential for several strategic industrial and defence imperatives. It will cost several hundred crore of rupees, but this is small change compared to national budgets, or even the substantial profits of a large corporate group.

Will the Tatas, by themselves or in a public–private partnership, summon up the will to make the world's fastest supercomputer, the dream with which this voyage began? Only time will tell. Perhaps this will require breakthrough cost-effective technology of a new kind, but more than ever it will require vision and courage.

What is clear, though, is that EKA was 'one of its kind', and it heralded a new era for India.

Tetley Enters the Tata Fold

*'Daring ideas are like chessmen moved forward. They may be
beaten, but they may start a winning game.'*

—Johann Wolfgang von Goethe

*'I knew a new world architecture was in the offing, and I knew we
had to respond. Tea is a universal drink, loved by every race and
nation. So if walls between countries were breaking down, we had
to respond by going global.'*

—R.K. Krishna Kumar

The fall of the Berlin Wall

In 1987, President Ronald Reagan of the United States had
challenged his Soviet counterpart Mikhail Gorbachev to 'tear
down this wall'.

On 9 November 1989, crowds of very excited Germans from
both sides climbed on to the wall with their sledgehammers.
They wanted to literally demolish the most visible manifestation
of the Iron Curtain. After the wall fell, the party continued late
into the night with revellers drinking champagne, sitting amidst
the debris. A euphoric public streamed through jubilantly,
crossing a boundary that was earlier a strip of death.

Watching this development keenly was a veteran of the Tata

Group, R.K. Krishna Kumar. Managing director of Tata Tea at the time, called Krishna by his senior colleagues and KK by the rest of the group, he felt in his bones that this was a defining moment. He says:

> The fall of the Berlin Wall signalled a new world structure, with no barriers. It laid open a flatter world where people would come together and dance without inhibition on a single great floor. For corporates like ourselves, country geographies would no longer be sacrosanct boundaries. Societies and economies would soon begin thinking beyond these barriers. This piece of writing was certainly on the wall.

KK's views were reinforced during his travels to the Soviet Union. As the Communist empire progressively disintegrated, he visited the Russian town of Sochi, which lies on the sweeping coastline of the Black Sea. This resort town is located close to the tea-growing areas of Georgia and is home to reputed tea packaging companies. There was newfound optimism among the people and the exciting red of Coca Cola was rapidly replacing the staid Communist crimson.

Tata Tea: From bush to cup

In 1989, Tata Tea was primarily a tea plantation company, confined to the shores of India. I had just joined the company and the corridor talk was flush with the colourful jargon of tea growers. Discussions centred on the virtues of plucking two leaves and a bud and exotic names such as broken orange pekoe tea were commonplace. There was considerable talk about the influence of crops and monsoons over tea price fluctuations and how this caused great anxiety at all levels of the company. It appeared that the revenues and profits of this business were at the mercy of the weather gods.

We were of course proud of the company's rolling plantations in the scenic Kanan Devan Hills of Kerala, and the lush green tea estates on the banks of the mighty Brahmaputra River in Assam. They produced fine teas of all types and were tended to with passion and care by able plantation staff and pluckers.

In the late 1980s, Tata Tea had begun taking steps to break some walls of its own, making forays beyond the boundaries of these plantations into branded tea. The driving idea here was that brands provided stability to the business, and would therefore help reduce the anxieties caused by widely fluctuating tea prices. This strategic effort was envisioned and led by Darbari Seth, who was chairman of the company, and by KK, who was heading the plantation divisions at the time.

The company launched two major brands: Kanan Devan and Tata Tea. These were brands with a big difference, because they contained 'plantation polypacked' tea. For the first time ever in the country, the teas were packaged on the estates while they were very fresh. 'Polypacks' were laminates of polyester and polythene, with very high barrier properties that kept both air and moisture out. The combination of plantation packing and polypacks ensured that consumers got very fresh tea.

By the mid-1990s, these brands had transformed the branded tea market in India. Tata Tea said 'Asli taazgi' (Real freshness) in its advertisements, consumers made a beeline for its packets and they loved what they drank. One particularly appealing advertisement of that period was based on a racy Hindi film song, and featured the vivacious Indian actress Anu Agarwal in a green dress, to reflect the colour of fresh tea leaves. It showed hundreds of thirsty men appealing to her for a sip of very fresh tea using a memorable Hindi line, 'Anu, Taazgi De De.' Their request was of course was immediately catered to, with cups of Tata Tea!

In addition, the company followed up on this spectacular success by launching a slew of other immensely successful brands, such as Chakra Gold and Agni. These brands were positioned on key attributes such as taste and strength, complementing the freshness platform of the plantation packed brands. Borrowing a phrase from Elvis Presley, Tata Tea's brand portfolio was now rocking.

Soon, the global giant Unilever, which had been an unchallenged market leader in India for several decades, was facing intense heat from Tata Tea, to the extent that it lost market share to Tata Tea. Within a decade, Tata Tea had captured 15 per cent of the market, second only to Unilever.

Percy Siganporia, who worked with KK for several years and would eventually rise to head the company, recalls that his computer screensaver in those days was 'Drink a pint of Unilever blood every day'. It bounced around on his screen endlessly, and many of his managers also adopted it as their mission. More than anything else, this slightly gory statement symbolized the company's aggressive stance in India.

Tata Tea also strove for thought leadership of the Indian tea market through brands based on new ideas. These were exciting times, and the company soon began riding a wave of rapid growth.

The global search

In the midst of such energetic activity and success in India, KK continued to quietly contemplate the implications of the fall of the Berlin Wall, and the imperative of going global. He knew that success in India was not deep enough to sustain the company for ever. His intense search for the next big breakthrough resulted in the formation of three major themes.

First, while Tata Tea had grown rapidly in India over the past decade, there was a natural limit to such growth. The company's market share would stabilize at some point in the future, even if it seized market leadership from Unilever. Thereafter, growth would be more gradual—India alone could not guarantee fast growth forever, making growth beyond the shores of India very important. It was also important because a flat world with disappearing boundaries meant that other big global players in tea, such as Twinings and Tetley, would soon attack Tata Tea's Indian stronghold.

Second, to grow beyond India, the biggest challenges were in building strong brands and establishing good distribution networks. Here again, there were limits to what the Tata brand alone could achieve in countries outside India. On the other hand, building a new brand overseas was not merely expensive but risky as well. Why would consumers in Europe or America accept an Indian brand? Why would supermarkets in those mature markets stock a new brand? In fact, a few years earlier, KK had undertaken a detailed study of the possibility of launching Tata Tea in the USA, and the risks appeared to outweigh the rewards.

The third theme was the distant possibility of acquiring an international tea brand. If this could be done, the risk of establishing a new brand would vanish immediately. This needed a brave new vision and, equally important, it required huge amounts of capital.

KK says, 'Vision often makes its first appearance disguised as a pipe dream. This has happened several times over in the history of the Tata Group. It is the true calling of leadership to seize such dreams, wake up quickly, and transform them into splendid reality.'

Testing the global waters

In the midst of these streams of thought, there were also some initial forays outside India, mostly during the early 1990s.

For several years, Tata Tea operated a subsidiary company called Tata Tea Inc. in Florida, which processed and resold instant tea to companies in the United States. The raw instant tea used here was supplied from Tata Tea's factory located in the Kanan Devan plantations. The American companies who bought from Tata Tea Inc. used the instant tea to make iced tea mixes, which they sold to retail consumers. Tata Tea Inc. built a relatively small but successful industrial business, but it had no consumer brands of its own.

Tata Tea also established a small joint venture with Hitachi of Japan to tap the Japanese tea and coffee market. While some interesting products were created, this experiment met with limited success.

Tata Tea, along with a Sri Lankan partner, bid successfully to acquire the famous Watawala Plantations of that country. This joint venture performed admirably, building a strong position in Sri Lanka and creating innovative brands such as Zesta and Watawala Kahata.

When viewed on a global canvas, these successes and failures appear minor but, in retrospect, they are like prologues to the main act. They speak volumes of the company's burning desire to go global, a desire that was soon to come of age.

Visitors in the Kanan Devan Hills

In 1991, an interesting group of people reached Tata Tea's plantations in the Kanan Devan Hills. They first headed to Ladbroke House, a splendid bungalow that nestles amidst the verdant estates. Leading this group was Stephen Alexander, chairman of Lyons Tetley. Accompanying him was a four-member senior team from both Britain and the Americas. Lyons Tetley was part of the large Allied Lyons group, which had a presence in foods, tea, coffee and breweries.

Receiving them at Ladbroke House were Darbari Seth, chairman of Tata Tea, and KK, who had by then assumed the role of managing director of the company. For two entire days, the teams travelled together around the plantations on a small bus, exchanging notes on a number of areas. I was a young manager on that bus, helping coordinate the visit and carefully observing the flow of conversation.

The Lyons Tetley team had bought instant teas from Tata Tea's subsidiary company in Florida and appreciated the excellent quality of the teas. Both companies were now keen on exploring a long-term strategic sourcing relationship. Stephen Alexander and his America point man, Henry 'Hank' McInerney, had a plan for a big launch of Tetley ready-to-drink iced teas in the USA, with flavours ranging from lemon to strawberry and peach. They were now searching for a steady source of good quality instant teas for this effort.

They were impressed by what they saw in the Kanan Devan Hills. As they walked around the plantations, the tea manufacturing units and the Nullatanni instant tea factory with its tall, spray-drying tower, they marvelled at the absolute commitment to quality. I recall Stephen Alexander being effusive in his praise after a brief visit to the Chundavurrai tea factory located at the top of the hills.

They were also equally impressed with the quality of Tata management. Darbari Seth and KK were masters of their art, and Stephen appeared to be particularly impressed with the commitment to excellent execution which was visible everywhere. I remember a statement he made to his colleagues, which I noted down carefully: 'KK is on top-of-line management here, and he gets things done. That's important, because we have to deal with him.' The visit culminated in a long-term strategic agreement for supply of instant teas to Tetley in the USA.

As an added bonus, it also resulted in the birth of a joint venture company, Tata Tetley Limited, which would manufacture teabags for export to specific Tetley markets. The unit was set up in the south Indian city of Kochi, the first bridge between two leading tea organizations. It built operational links at various levels. The foundation stone of trust had been laid down between the senior teams of Tata Tea and Lyons Tetley. It wasn't unlike Henry Kissinger's first visit to China, which opened lines of frank communication at the highest levels—key to any endeavour that spans different continents and cultures.

Reflecting on this, KK says, 'I instantly knew we had found a pathway to going global, which was absolutely critical to our future. The chemistry was very good, and Tetley was a great global brand. But we still had to learn how exactly to traverse that path.'

Getting to know Tetley

Soon thereafter, a Tata Tea team reciprocated the visit, and toured Tetley facilities in the UK and the USA. I was privileged to be part of this team. We met several important people at the Tetley headquarters in Greenford near London, and also at New Jersey in the USA. We were very impressed with what we saw.

The Tetley brand was legendary. It traced its origins to the merchants Joseph and Edward Tetley, who had established a tea business in Yorkshire in 1837. A few years later, they relocated to London and established Joseph Tetley & Company, Wholesale Tea Dealers. Soon, Tetley had become England's favourite cup of tea.

Tetley was the first company that launched teabags in the UK, in 1953. Teabags are commonplace today, but at the time of launch they were a breakthrough product that had completely transformed the experience of brewing and drinking tea. Later, Tetley also launched the revolutionary 'round teabags', as an alternative to the square teabags that were in use. With warm and memorable advertising that highlighted several virtues of the round shape, this new product further cemented Tetley's formidable reputation among tea-drinking consumers.

Over the years, Tetley successfully expanded its presence across the West, eventually including the entire UK, Europe, Canada, Russia and Australia in its markets. It quickly took its place in the upper echelons of the consideration of tea drinkers in those markets. Globally, it was second only to Lipton.

We also toured and saw the excellent facilities and capabilities that Tetley possessed in the buying, blending and manufacture of tea. At the headquarters in Greenford, we saw how carefully tea blends were created and verified for quality.

Over the next few years, the teams would get to know each other better. They would happily discover that both companies were fully committed to the world of tea, and also that they shared some important common values. The dating had begun, though there was no marriage on the horizon, yet.

The first bid for Tetley

Four years later, the first serious proposal was on the cards.

In 1994, Allied Lyons, owners of the Tetley brand, had merged with Pedro Domecq to create a huge liquor and retailing multinational, which was christened Allied Domecq. This merged company owned a number of famous liquor brands such as Ballantine's Whisky, Beefeater Gin, Teacher's Highland Cream Whisky, Kahlua coffee liqueur and Courvoisier Cognac.

A year later in 1995, Allied Domecq decided to focus on its large liquor business, and to exit the non-core tea and coffee business. It announced its intention to divest the Tetley tea and coffee brands.

At Tata Tea, when KK heard this news, he was immediately interested in pursuing the purchase of Tetley. The global search had remained uppermost in his mind, and the Tetley brand could catapult the company into this space instantly. This was a rare opportunity; it had to be seized with both hands. Of course, Tetley was much larger than Tata Tea; the funds required for such an acquisition would be staggering.

Notwithstanding these issues, KK was supported in his enthusiasm by senior directors of the Tata Group, including Darbari Seth and Noshir Soonawala, who had been chairman and deputy chairman respectively of Tata Tea for several years, and by Ratan Tata, who had become chairman of the Tata Group in 1991. They saw the compelling logic of going global, and felt the opportunity deserved to be explored.

A Tata Tea team reached London in early 1995 to pursue the acquisition. The team pitched camp at the elegant St James' Court Hotel, located very close to Buckingham Palace. Various documents and files relating to Tetley were studied in a pre-appointed room in central London, over countless prawn sandwiches and cups of tea. The objective was to understand the company in greater detail.

There were also extensive discussions with the Allied Domecq team, with senior members of the Tetley management and with bankers who could potentially fund the acquisition. Some of these talks stretched past midnight. Consensus was achieved on a number of fronts, but the prolonged sessions on financing the acquisition got mired in several details. Tata Tea struggled to put in place the finance for the acquisition arrangements required. In retrospect, this was not surprising, given that it was the first instance of an Indian company attempting to acquire such a large global brand.

Meanwhile a management buy-in team, backed by some venture capitalist firms, was also keenly pursuing Tetley. This team was led by the entrepreneur Leon Allen, who brought with him the earlier experience of acquiring and selling the canned juice brand, Del Monte. He was supported in the bid by two investment firms, Schroder Ventures and Prudential Venture Management. They pulled ahead of Tata Tea by quickly putting together the funding required for the purchase. With this strength, their negotiations progressed confidently and successfully.

In June 1995, Allied Domecq announced the sale of the Tetley tea business to this venture capital funded team. Tata Tea had come so close to achieving its global dream, but unfortunately had not made it to the finish line.

KK recalls that moment in London:

> We felt sad. We could not achieve certainty on our financial plan, so our offer had been rejected. But I think we gained a great deal by participating in this bid. Very importantly, we realized that we had to get our act together on our funding arrangements well in advance, if we ever desired to make such a large global acquisition. It was a lesson well learnt.

Tetley is up for sale again

KK and his colleagues in the Tata Group felt that the venture capitalist firms which had bought Tetley had only a medium-term interest in the company. The reason was simple. Schroder and Prudential were financial investors and had no strategic or deep commitment to the tea industry. In other words, they would want to sell their stake in the company very soon.

This day came sooner than expected. In February 1999, KK received a call from the global financial and management consulting firm, Arthur Andersen. 'The owners of Tetley are willing to sell. They prefer a buyer who has long-term interests in tea. Would Tata Tea be interested?'

KK knew that this was a defining moment once again, a moment that required resolute and quick action. He had studied history well enough to know that such moments come rarely. When they do, they have to be seized quickly and fully. He spoke to Ratan Tata and to Noshir Soonawala at the Tata Group headquarters. The essential logic for acquiring Tetley was clear to all of them.

1. This acquisition would provide Tata Tea a giant leap on to the global canvas.
2. This was a one-time opportunity to acquire a leading global brand of tea with a presence in thirty-five countries.
3. No other brand of this size was likely to be on sale in the near future. Building a new brand of such stature was expensive, very risky and virtually impossible.
4. Tetley also provided access to a well-established global distribution network.
5. Tata Tea and Tetley had complementary strengths. Tata Tea was strong in packet teas and developing countries such as India and the Middle East. On the other hand, Tetley had unrivalled expertise in teabags, in developed countries including the UK, USA, Canada and Europe.

There were several potential synergies of the acquisition. Tetley and Tata Tea could source their teas together, thus deriving economies of capability and scale. A global manufacturing and supply chain could drive costs down. The Tetley brand could be launched in India, Russia and other Asian markets, appealing to the premium end of the market.

Finally, both companies were passionate about tea and fully committed to this beverage. The strength of the resultant combined entity would be a powerful foundation on which a giant global tea enterprise could be built. The acquisition itself was expected to be a daunting challenge.

Show me the money!

Tata Tea was much smaller than Tetley. At that time, the net worth of Tata Tea was around US$115 million, which was less than one-third the net worth of Tetley. Even in terms of sales revenues, Tata Tea was half the size of Tetley. How could Tata Tea then have the audacity to even consider purchasing a company that was several times its size? Would such a purchase create unbearable indigestion and risk for Tata Tea?

Then there was the hurdle that had tripped up Tata Tea in 1995. The funds required would be formidable, certainly in the range of hundreds of millions of dollars. Where would the money come from?

A third issue was that this acquisition essentially centred on acquiring the famous brand Tetley. Indian companies were comfortable acquiring brick-and-mortar assets abroad, such as factories and machines which could be seen and touched. But buying an intangible asset that lived only in the minds of people created a zone of discomfort. Were there hidden or unknown risks lurking here?

The cultural factor was equally important. Tetley was a blue-blooded British company and brand, with rich heritage. Tata

Tea was a proud Indian company, with an equally rich but very different history of its own. Would integration between these two diverse cultures ever be possible?

The poet Rudyard Kipling had once written 'Oh, east is east, and west is west, and never the twain shall meet.' Could Tata Tea and Tetley find a meeting point, or would this chasm between cultures pose yet another hurdle for the acquisition?

We shall find a way

A pioneer has to find the way around challenges that appear insurmountable, because he is attempting to scale a peak that has never been conquered before. Tata Tea demonstrated this spirit, when, in the months of March and April 1999, it carefully considered all these challenges and then decided to make a renewed bid to acquire Tetley.

KK says that all the answers were not yet at hand. But he knew that, with the unstinting support of Ratan Tata, Noshir Soonawala and the Tata Group, 'we shall find a way'. After all, he says, this is what the founder Jamsetji Tata had repeatedly done, when he had established Tata Steel in an underdeveloped part of India or created the Taj Mahal Hotel at Apollo Bunder in Mumbai. He concludes that corporate courage often comes from knowing that the path being taken is correct, sensitive to history and in harmony with the broad sweep of trends.

In April 1999, Tata Tea appointed Arthur Andersen as financial advisers to the proposed acquisition of Tetley, signalling its serious intent. At the Mumbai offices of Arthur Andersen, an initial study was undertaken to determine the financial value of Tetley.

I participated in those sessions where we pored over some initial business plans that had been made available. Leading our study team was Percy Siganporia, the Tata Tea veteran who had the macabre fantasy of sipping Unilever blood. We were caught up in the sheer excitement of being part of a historic voyage, and the lights burned well past midnight.

During these discussions, the Arthur Andersen consultants offered us their inputs, and alternative valuation techniques were used to assess a range of financial metrics. We also revalidated that the strategy underlying the acquisition was correct. We then prepared a detailed presentation covering all these aspects.

In June 1999, the board of directors of Tata Tea, headed by Ratan Tata, heard out this presentation and discussed the subject in detail. This meeting was held in the stately wood-panelled boardroom of Bombay House. The room is located at one end of the fourth floor, which also houses the offices of the chairman. All these years later, I am still overwhelmed when I enter these chambers through the tall wooden doors set with large, round brass knobs. Appropriately enough, a marble bust of the pioneering founder, Jamsetji Tata, sits at one end of this august room. I am sure he would have been delighted to hear the conversation that took place that day.

In a milestone decision, the board of directors agreed with the strategic rationale for the acquisition of Tetley. It also approved the submission of an indicative offer to the owners of Tetley, thereby moving into the next stage of the acquisition process. A historic ball had just been set in motion.

The Tata team at Greenford, London

Once a tentative bid had been submitted, there were two important tasks to be undertaken. Tata Tea had to verify that the brand and business they wanted to buy was in good health.

Simultaneously, they needed to finalize an approach to the critical matter of funding the acquisition.

The verification process is commonly called due diligence, because the buyer exercises due diligence by studying all the details provided by the seller. This covers a mass of details relating to the brands, the factories and the people, as well as various commercial and legal issues. It is a comprehensive process, requires the reading and review of several thousand documents and takes several weeks to complete.

I was part of the due diligence team that was headed by Percy Siganporia. The due diligence rooms were located within the Tetley premises at Greenford in London. Representatives of Arthur Andersen accompanied us. Also guiding the process was Arun Gandhi, a leading Indian authority on mergers and acquisitions. Gandhi was a partner of the accounting firm N.M. Raiji at the time. With his approval, a team from Rabobank, a large Dutch bank that had been identified as a potential banker to the acquisition, undertook their own independent study of the business. An arm of Deloitte & Touche, the global consulting and audit firm, studied accounting and structural issues.

This team was in constant communication with KK, discussing findings and their impact on the valuation of Tetley. The Tata Tea team studied data and travelled to various countries including the USA and Canada to assess Tetley facilities and markets. It asked searching questions of the Tetley management. It insisted on responses, firmly yet politely.

Percy Siganporia says his team and he had to be ambassadors of the Tata Group, therefore the way they conducted themselves during the due diligence exercise was very important.

'We were from India, a different cultural setting. The eyes of the Tetley management were constantly upon us. Every individual conversation was important. We had to work with absolute transparency. We also knew this was the first time a Tata team was undertaking such an effort on a global scale, which made us particularly responsible.'

He also remembers that the effort ran into several roadblocks, which had to be gently navigated each time. He narrates one such event:

> One fine morning, when we reached the Tetley due diligence room, we heard that news of Tata Tea acquiring Tetley had appeared in Indian newspapers. Ken Pringle and Peter Unsworth, who headed Tetley, took great umbrage to this news leak, and perhaps rightly so. They told me that the inaccurate reports which had appeared damaged the process. They implied that we were responsible, because the leak had happened somewhere in India. And they refused to provide us any further data. For several days, they shut the door on us, stopped the acquisition process, and there was no further conversation.
>
> This was at a critical point in our study of Tetley. We could have left the Tetley premises and returned to India. But we stayed put at Greenford. We wanted Ken and Peter to know that shutting the door was not a break from our viewpoint. We were very serious about progressing the deal. So the next time they opened the door, we would still be there on the doorstep, with our list of questions.

This specific matter was eventually resolved through high-level dialogue. But Siganporia notes that such a persistent, professional approach led to a great deal of mutual respect between the Tetley and Tata Tea teams.

Perhaps this also led to trust and some fondness setting in. On Christmas Eve 1999, as the due diligence was drawing to a close, the Tetley team, led by Pringle and Unsworth, walked down to the rooms occupied by Siganporia and his boys. They wished them a merry Christmas and spoke of how much they admired the quality of due diligence work. In an unexpected gesture, they also gifted the Tata Tea team quaint ceramic figures of the 'Tetley tea folk'. These are warm, animated characters which had been used in the Tetley tea advertising in the UK. Gaffer is the head of the Tetley tea folk, a perfectionist who believes in making the best cup of tea. His colleague Sydney is a kind and gentle fellow, always on hand with a cup of tea during moments of crisis. Other tea folk include Maurice, Clarenze, Gordon, Tina and Archie. Accompanying these gifts were small, personalized cards that carried warm words and wishes.

Funding the acquisition of Tetley

The due diligence process established that the Tetley business was in good health. It helped Tata Tea understand the Tetley organization. It also highlighted specific points of concern that had to be addressed. Back in his office in Mumbai, KK was consumed with the contours of a viable funding package and structure for the acquisition. The painful memories of 1995 were still vivid.

Most historic events are marked by a few turning points that determine their eventual course. The history of the Second World War throws up the siege of Leningrad, the Battle of Britain, the landings at Normandy and the atomic bombing of Japan as inflection points that resulted in the Allied victory.

There were three similar turning points that enabled funding for the acquisition of Tetley and thus opened the doors for global acquisitions by Indian companies.

First, Tata Sons, the parent company of the Tata Group,

provided its full backing to this pioneering move by Tata Tea.
This was powerful currency, because of the trust that the Tata
name commanded in the financial community. In a networked
world, European and American banks were fully aware of the
Tata Group, its size and strength in India, its strong
management and its impeccable track record.

KK says, 'Ratan Tata's courage to draft and back gigantic
transactions was the key to the Tetley deal. Many people develop
cold feet when faced with a deal of this size, particularly when
no Indian company had gone this route before. But he stood
his ground and provided his unstinted support, and that made
all the difference.'

A second turning point that KK remembers fondly was a
meeting with a senior team from Rabobank. A Dutch bank
that is among the largest and safest financial institutions in the
world, Rabobank had traditionally focused on food and
agribusiness, so tea naturally belonged to their world. However,
it had a fledgling presence in India at that time.

KK narrates with relish the story of this decisive moment:

> I was deep in the midst of addressing the financing challenge,
> when a Rabobank team came to meet me in my office at the
> Taj Mahal Hotel. There was Wouter J. Kolff, vice-chairman of
> Rabobank International. Accompanying him was Rana
> Kapoor, who represented the bank in India.
>
> The topic of conversation turned to Indian companies and
> their global ambitions. I knew Rabobank was small in India,
> but I seized the opportunity to mention to them the Tetley
> opportunity. I told him that such an acquisition could
> transform not merely Tata Tea, but the very manner in which
> Indian companies looked at the world outside.
>
> But this is a big deal, and it needs the right financial backup
> running into over 250 million British pounds, I added. Wouter

Kolff looked me in the eye for a few seconds. Then, he stood up, shook hands very firmly, and said, 'Done.'

At that moment, I knew that two trustworthy partners had come together. Looking at his body language, I also knew that Rabobank would make this happen. It was a turning point.

Rabobank would go on to play a very important role as lead banker, manager and arranger for the Tetley acquisition. It delivered superbly on the deal, despite initial scepticism in some quarters that a bank with such a small presence in India could do so. Rana Kapoor, in particular, played a critical role. He served as a close and valued partner, and walked all the way, even covering the last mile where the final few gaps in financing had to be filled.

The third and equally important turning point was the clever financial structuring of the acquisition. Here, Noshir Soonawala, finance director of Tata Sons, was a valuable guide and architect. Known to possess a razor-sharp intellect, he helped develop the framework that made the deal possible. KK and he had formed a close personal friendship over several years, so they must have thoroughly enjoyed working together on this challenge.

They soon concluded that, given the large size of funding required, the acquisition should be undertaken through a leveraged buyout (LBO). An LBO uses a significant amount of borrowed money, either bonds or loans, to acquire a company. It permits companies to make large acquisitions without committing a lot of capital in the initial period.

For the Tetley acquisition, the borrowings amounted to over 75 per cent of the bid price. This enabled Tata Tea, a relatively small company, to undertake such a massive purchase. The Tata Group's backing was of course critical in convincing overseas bankers to loan these large amounts.

There was another interesting angle to the financial structure evolved by Soonawala and the Tata Group. They safeguarded the interests of Tata Tea by ensuring that the future cash flows of Tetley, the company being acquired, formed the collateral for these borrowings. In the jargon of financiers, Tetley was 'ring-fenced'. This colourful term is derived from the ring-fencing of farms, which helps keep cattle and other livestock within its boundaries. In a similar manner, such financial transactions keep loans, as well as the liabilities which arise from such borrowings, within clear boundaries.

This was achieved by the creation of a separate legal entity in the UK. To begin with, Tata Tea invested equity capital and established this new company. The company then borrowed the remainder of the funds required. The equity capital and borrowings constituted the total funding needed to carry out the acquisition.

A historic moment

Tata Tea was now in a position to submit a final bid for Tetley. In January 2000, there were hectic and involved discussions to determine the final bid price.

The conclusions of the due diligence were considered at this stage. Arthur Andersen helped draw a post-acquisition road map and business plan. Several alternative valuation approaches, common in the world of mergers and acquisitions, were used to determine exactly how much could be paid for acquiring Tetley.

Without getting into technical details, suffice to say that these approaches included a net present value analysis, which looked at the current value of future cash streams. Also included was a study of comparable transactions in the past, as well as a review of the value of existing foods and beverages companies that are listed on various stock exchanges. In addition, Rabobank carried out a separate valuation of Tetley as well.

Based on all these inputs, KK and the Tata Group decided on the final price that they would bid for Tetley. The figure they converged on was GBP 271 million. A leveraged buyout of this type was unheard of in India at the time.

Tata Tea was on the verge of making history. Matters now moved rapidly to meet the timelines specified by the owners of Tetley. This was important, because if these dates were not met, other bidders could enter the fray too.

There were presentations to potential bankers, to convince them of the merits of the acquisition. Rabobank, the lead arrangers, coordinated this effort. There were also a host of legal and statutory matters to be handled.

The final bid, fully backed by financing, was submitted to the owners and then accepted. This was a defining and historic moment. Tata Tea had created history by acquiring a global brand and business several times its size. It had created history for itself, for the Tata Group and for India.

A celebratory dinner at the Bombay Brasserie

On the day the acquisition was completed, KK hosted a celebratory dinner in London for the Tata Tea team, including its advisers from Arthur Andersen, N.M. Raiji and Rabobank. The venue was the Bombay Brasserie, a swanky Indian restaurant located in the fashionable Kensington area. The restaurant promises its patrons the flavours of India and Bombay.

It was quite appropriate that a journey which began in Bombay House was now being toasted at the Bombay Brasserie.

There were smiles and bonhomie all around, and champagne flowed. Percy Siganporia and I were seated next to each other at this dinner. I think our eyes were moist, and those tears owed nothing to the spicy lamb curry we relished that evening.

When we left the restaurant well past midnight, snowflakes were falling softly, all around. The night was silent and calm.

Tetley in the Tata fold

When the Tetley acquisition was announced, there was exuberance and applause. Indian media saluted this as a path-breaking initiative for the country. The world cheered and took notice of an Indian company that had the chutzpah to successfully bid for a global company much bigger than itself.

But immediately thereafter, there was work to be done. The coming together of the two companies would pose several challenges and opportunities. A big opportunity was extracting synergies from the acquisition. A big challenge was ensuring integration of the two businesses and teams. This was particularly important, given the diverse cultures involved. In addition, the level of borrowings involved in the leveraged buyout had to be gradually reduced, which was essential to de-risk the business.

Each of these areas was successfully addressed, and how this was accomplished is a separate story in itself. The Tetley deal also gave Tata Tea the confidence to undertake other smaller acquisitions in the years that followed. The single biggest task of course was the fusion of all these businesses into a single global entity. This moment was reached in the year 2008, when the formation of Tata Global Beverages encompassing Tetley, Tata Tea and other acquired companies and joint ventures was announced by KK at a company conference held in Prague.

The Tetley and Tata Tea brands continue to blaze a trail of growth and progress. Their appeal to consumers in over forty countries has only grown stronger with the years. There are many new challenges, including an economic slowdown in Europe and the Americas, as well as changing consumer preferences. But the hunger for growth, which was so evident in the acquisition of Tetley, remains undiminished.

Lessons from the Tetley acquisition

The Tetley acquisition was a path-breaking venture because it created new opportunities for the Tata Group and other reputed Indian firms. A key lesson learnt was that while financing is a formidable task, it can be accomplished smartly and with manageable risk.

It also threw open for Tata companies the power and possibilities inherent in the Tata name. This has clearly played an important role in later global forays of the group, including the recent acquisitions of Corus and Jaguar Land Rover.

It showed India that it is possible to achieve audacious dreams. Many more Berlin Walls can be broken down, if pursued tenaciously with head and heart.

Tata Steel Wins the Deming Prize

'Quality is not an act. It is a habit.'

—Aristotle

'One must forever strive for excellence, or even perfection, in any task, however small, and never be satisfied with the second best.'

—J.R.D. Tata

A midnight call from Japan

On 6 October 2008, a 3 a.m. phone call woke B. Muthuraman, managing director of Tata Steel, up in Chicago. He heard a distant Japanese voice, speaking in English. Due to the marked difference in accents it normally takes some time to comprehend the Japanese, even when one is wide awake. In the dead of the night, the challenge must have been even greater.

Muthuraman recalls that conversation:

> I recognized the Japanese person on the call as one of the assessors who had visited our company earlier in the year. He told me, very simply and directly, that Tata Steel had been awarded the Deming Prize. This is a most coveted quality award that companies across the world crave for. I wasn't sure

whether I had heard him correctly. I was not entirely awake, he was speaking in halting Japanese English, and this was phenomenal news. I just said 'Thank you', and the call was over.

But the news was too good to be true, so I wanted to call him back immediately, just to verify what he had actually said. Then I felt it would be stupid to do this. My wife, who was next to me, had been woken up by all this noise, and asked me what this was all about. I shared the news with her, and then rang up my senior colleague Hemant Nerurkar at Jamshedpur. Of course I could not sleep any more. The phone rang many more times that night. Because we had won.

Muthuraman would go on to win many other honours, including the Padma Bhushan bestowed by the President of India. However, he considers the Deming Prize to be very special.

This award is for the organization. It is for the effort of some 35,000 people of Tata Steel. Only if these 35,000 people are sharply aligned towards a common goal and committed to the highest levels of quality, will you be able to win the Deming Prize. A collective effort such as this is always more challenging, more rewarding than awards and prizes for individual efforts. I felt proud for all our people. This was a dream come true.

Tata Steel had become the first steel company outside Japan to be awarded the Deming Prize. It was the culmination of several years of single-minded commitment to the principle of business excellence and total quality management (TQM). The steel mill that Jamsetji Tata had established in the wild jungles of eastern India, more than a century ago, had made India proud once again.

William Edward Deming was a celebrated American

statistician, professor and author. It is interesting to note that the Deming Prize is not awarded by his homeland but by the Japanese Union of Scientists and Engineers (JUSE). Japan is well known for its extreme commitment to quality, which is why brands like Toyota and Sony command such loyalty across the world. William Deming is celebrated in Japan, because he spent a considerable amount of time teaching the Japanese the key principles of statistical quality control. This prize was instituted to honour him for his invaluable contributions, which the Japanese believed were a cornerstone of their global success. In 1960, Deming was also awarded Japan's Order of the Sacred Treasure.

The Deming Prize (earlier known as the Deming Application Prize) is one of the most difficult awards to challenge and win. Here is what the Deming Prize Committee says, even as it describes some characteristics of potential winners: 'There is no easy success in these times of change. Companies need to think on their own, set lofty goals, and drive themselves to challenge and achieve these goals.' The committee looks for companies that not only improve their businesses but also transform them through TQM.

The Deming Prize Committee is customarily chaired by the chairman of the Japanese Federation of Economic Organizations (Keidanren). A steering group and three committees, each consisting of quality experts from industry and academia, carry out a rigorous examination of applicant companies.

For a company as large as Tata Steel to win the prize is even more extraordinary, since this meant that TQM principles and their applications had been adopted across several thousand people spanning multiple shop floors and locations.

The quality movement at Tata Steel

The story begins several years ago, in the late 1980s. Tata Steel had just begun sowing the seeds of TQM under the leadership of Dr J.J. Irani and B. Muthuraman. Both of them visited Japan on missions to understand how that country had created world-beating companies using quality as a key tool. They came back enthused and convinced that the Japanese methods needed to be replicated back home.

Their early efforts, initiated in Tata Steel's sprawling factory at Jamshedpur, included the concept of quality circles. Each circle consisted of several managers and workers, who would gather near their shop floors to discuss specific quality concepts and issues. These teams would then try to develop specific solutions and improvements. The quality circles would cover many subjects: product quality, productivity, cost and safety. Over the next two decades the number of quality circles grew to over 7500, covering an astonishing 96 per cent of the company's employees. Few companies had stretched so far and wide.

Around the same time, ISO standards defined by the International Organization for Standardization were also implemented in various parts of the company. These certifications helped drive and enforce consistency, a hallmark of quality.

A focused programme called TOP—Total Operations Performance—was launched. This engaged high-calibre employees with the task of coming up with new ideas and delivering quick results. Tata Steel also wholeheartedly embraced two prominent schools of thought in the area of quality improvement—Juran and Kaizen.

In the Juran methodology, established by the American quality evangelist Joseph M. Juran, companies address the cost of poor quality and work on eliminating the root causes that lead to such lapses. Kaizen, on the other hand, was actively implemented in Japan after the Second World War, and focuses on continuous improvement or change for the better in every single aspect of business. In fact, the word Kaizen means 'improvement' in Japanese.

While the initial focus was on product quality, it soon transferred to quality in everything that the company undertook. This statement from Dr J.J. Irani, who was managing director of Tata Steel at that time, demonstrates this paradigm shift: 'Business excellence is much more than quality. In Tata Steel, we started by just talking about the quality of the product. Then we talked about the big Q, quality in all its facets, and the small q, which pertains to the quality of the product.'

Dr Irani, a large man himself, used the big 'Q' as a powerful weapon to transform Tata Steel from an ageing manufacturer of steel to a vibrant, efficient company that became the lowest-cost producer of steel in the world. All these efforts entailed strong commitment from the management, thousands of employees and the employees' union that represents the interests of the workforce. It instilled a belief across the company that it was possible to improve quality and productivity and to beat down cost and waste, all at the same time.

This shared quality consciousness became a very strong foundation on which the company could build its future efforts. Indeed, this is the origin of the 'sharp alignment among the 35,000 employees' that Muthuraman spoke about, while reflecting on his midnight telephone call and the Deming Prize. It was the biggest victory that Tata Steel had won for itself in this early phase of the quality movement because, without this widespread sense of ownership, no progress would have been possible.

Pursuit of business excellence

In the 1990s, after the initial bout of scrupulous experimentation with various improvement methods, Tata Steel actively began using the Malcolm Baldrige framework of quality and excellence, which originated in the USA. The Baldrige framework emphasizes organizational excellence, not restricting itself to product or service quality. The Malcolm Baldrige National Quality Award, based on this evaluation, is the only formal recognition of performance excellence of both public and private US organizations, awarded by the President of the USA.

Shortly thereafter, the Tata Group adopted the Malcolm Baldrige philosophy for all companies in the group. It established the Tata Business Excellence Model, popularly known as TBEM, within the group. TBEM covers seven pillars that are essential for excellence in any organization: leadership, strategy, customer focus, employee focus, processes, measurement and analysis and the results achieved by the company. The TBEM movement has become a way of life in several Tata companies today, and has contributed significantly to the successes they have achieved in their respective spheres of business.

In 1995, the Tata Group also announced the JRD Quality Value Award, shortened to JRD-QV Award. This award was instituted in memory of J.R.D. Tata. It would be awarded to Tata companies that crossed a high score of 600, after a detailed evaluation under the TBEM. Achieving such a high score in TBEM signified that the company had breached a very high barrier in its pursuit of excellence and perfection in business.

Ratan Tata explained why the Tata Group prefers to remember and immortalize J.R.D. Tata through this award: 'Considering that he adored perfection to such an extent that this was an intimate part of his life, I thought an annual award, the JRD Quality Value Award, would be a good way to remember him.'

The JRD-QV Award instantly became one of the most coveted recognitions in the Tata Group. Tata Steel immediately embraced TBEM, and became one of its foremost proponents. It also trained its sights on the JRD-QV Award.

At the heart of TBEM resides the vision of what the company wishes to be, and how this is relentlessly pursued by everyone in the team. Tata Steel defined a particular vision of becoming the lowest-cost steel producer in the world. Using a sound leadership system, it then translated this ambitious vision into specific strategies, as well as underlying processes that supported these strategies. Once again, it involved its entire workforce in this exciting but arduous journey.

To make all of this possible, a special team was formed in the managing director's office. Its only task was to drive quality and business excellence across Tata Steel. It reported directly to Dr Irani, who gave it the authority to drive change wherever required.

There were many disappointments along the way. In its very first assessment under TBEM, Tata Steel failed the test miserably. It recorded a very low score—less than 200 as against a maximum possible score of 1000. This was also light years away from the milestone score of 600 necessary to win the JRD-QV Award.

Avneesh Gupta, who led the quality journey at Tata Steel for many years recounts the early days:

> Of course we were dejected by the low score. There was serious debate among many of us on whether we are up to the mark, and also on whether we have been able to express everything we have done. Dr Irani was clear that we needed to

act, not just write a better TBEM application. He told us to listen to the people who had assessed us, and learn with an open mind. This is not just an examination, he said, it is a journey to improve.

Dr Irani re-emphasizes this point in an interview with Sujata Agarwal of the Tata Group:

> We tend to develop a frog-in-the-well attitude; we think everything around us is fine. And then somebody from the outside sees our business and points out flaws and we think that is unfair. That is the wrong attitude to take. We have to take cognizance because the people who made those comments are not spiteful. They honestly feel something is wrong.

The team at Tata Steel listened to the feedback; they worked hard to improve their practices, processes and systems. Every single year thereafter, they submitted a detailed application to be assessed under TBEM. The results began to speak for themselves. By 1997, the TBEM score had moved up to 443. In the 1998 assessment, Tata Steel scored 510. Finally, in 2000, Tata Steel recorded a score of 616, crossing the magic milestone of 600. It had become the first company in the Tata Group to qualify for the JRD-QV Award!

The JRD-QV Award and beyond

The JRD-QV awards function is held on 29 July each year, to mark the birth anniversary of J.R.D. Tata. The venue is usually the Jamshed Bhabha Theatre, in the elegant National Centre for Performing Arts (NCPA), located just off the Arabian Sea in south Mumbai. In 2000, as the new millennium dawned, a proud Tata Steel team led by Dr Irani received the award from Ratan Tata. The ovation that ensued never seemed to cease.

Avneesh Gupta, who was present on this momentous occasion, says, 'This was a moment of intense pride for all of us. I was there in NCPA. It was not just a heady moment; it felt like one more graduation day in college. And of course we had graduated into the next league!'

Tata Steel celebrated the JRD-QV Award, but it did not rest on its laurels. Immediately it began working towards the next target, a score that would shatter the 650-mark barrier.

Ratan Tata acknowledged and paid tribute to this philosophy of constant improvement at the next JRD-QV recognition function:

> Last year at this time, it was a matter of great happiness to see one of our companies finally win the JRD-QV Award. I think Jamshed [Dr Irani] and his team deserved every bit of the acknowledgement they received on that occasion.
>
> The Tata Steel people could have taken a holiday, a sabbatical from this whole process, since they knew they could not win the award again, that being what we had decided. But it is really gratifying to see that the company decided to stay with this process and work at it. As Jaggu [G. Jagannathan, who headed Tata Quality Management Services, the organization that leads and administers the TBEM process] said, this is a journey that really has no end.

In 2004, under the leadership of B. Muthuraman, who had taken over as managing director from Dr Irani, the company's TBEM score crossed 700—the highest score any Tata company had reached. It was remarkable that such progress had been achieved within four years of receiving the JRD-QV Award. Tata Steel received a special Leadership in Excellence plaque to mark this milestone.

The big question now staring Tata Steel in the face after all these TBEM milestones—what next?

The next leap forward

After winning the JRD-QV Award in 2000, Tata Steel brought the TOP programme out of its factory and into its marketing and sales offices. Programmes called 'customer value management' and 'retail value management' were launched, to streamline efforts towards retail customers.

In 2004, the company began work on using the Theory of Constraints, a concept introduced to the world of business by the legendary Dr Eliyahu Moshe Goldratt. In essence, he urged companies to identify the constraints that limit them, and to then remove them so that the business breaks free of them. Dr Goldratt's bestselling book *The Goal* illustrates this concept through a powerful story that is a delight to read.

Dr Goldratt, a charismatic person with a strong viewpoint, introduced his concepts to B. Muthuraman. He highlighted the huge business benefits that could result from identifying and raising the key constraint that held back Tata Steel's further progress. The supply chain was identified as a major area here, and Tata Steel has since then benefited significantly in various parts of its business by implementing the Theory of Constraints. This has included timely supplies of finished steel products to its customers and also intermediate planning at its mines and collieries, which is critical to the eventual manufacturing of steel.

This project required extreme patience and attention to detail, but it was clear that it had raised quality standards and output. Here is one typical instance. The washeries at Tata Steel were identified as a key constraint; they were causing a large percentage of product rejections. Washeries are the place where raw coal is washed before it is used in the manufacturing process. In order to counter the problem, a buffer of raw coal was set up before the washeries. This buffer enabled a more consistent supply of coal of more homogenous quality being fed to the washeries. The improved quality of input ensured that throughput through the washery was maintained. As a result, rejections came down and the output of the washeries went up.

Amidst all these improvements, the Tata Steel team was now once again raring to subject itself to a rigorous external assessment of its business. They had crossed a TBEM score of 700, and were well ahead of all the other Tata companies. Muthuraman felt that a new challenge was needed to guard against the risk of complacency setting in the team. They also felt that an external examination was important to break out of the 'frog-in-the-well' syndrome that Dr Irani had described so accurately. They knew that great companies create new challenges for themselves and also open themselves to outside scrutiny ever so often.

So, this time around, they chose to subject the company to the most challenging quality assessment, an examination for the Deming Prize.

Why Deming?

The Deming Prize is regarded as the highest award in the area of quality and total quality management, the Nobel Prize its closest contemporary. This makes Deming a singular achievement, to be cherished forever.

Every Deming applicant had to subject itself to one of the most rigorous quality examinations known to man. The Japanese examiners are tough as nails and as independent as the wind. Secondly, the Deming model emanates from the shop floor. It focuses on outstanding work on a daily basis, in each office and each manufacturing shop. One cannot get away only on the basis of great strategy. Daily work management is about conforming fully to strategy and to customer expectations in every corner of the company, and being very stable in this process.

For both these reasons, Tata Steel decided to open up the company to the Deming assessment.

There are only three questions in a Deming examination:

1. What challenging and customer-oriented business objectives and strategies have you established?
2. How have you gone about implementing the principles of TQM in achieving these planned objectives and strategies?
3. What are the outstanding results you have obtained as an outcome of these actions, compared to the defined objectives and strategies?

These questions appear disarmingly simple, but their answers require incredible precision and ambition.

To illustrate this point, assume you are an ace mountain climber with lofty goals. First, you have to set yourself a clear and ambitious objective—say, summiting Mount Everest. Lesser goals, such as climbing a local rock, will certainly not be acceptable.

Then, you have to define key strategies for this challenging climb: which face will you mount the ascent from and why, will you undertake the climb solo or in a group, what kind of people will you have in your group, would you first climb a lesser mountain to prepare yourself for Everest, and many other questions.

Thereafter, you need to define a very systematic climbing plan, aligned to these goals and strategies. This has to include a detailed timeline for the ascent, including adequate resources of every kind, knowledge of every crag and the most dangerous stretches, lessons from the experiences of previous climbers who have succeeded and failed and weather conditions based on past data and meteorological projections. It also has to include a plan of preparing fully for abnormalities, say an unexpected heavy avalanche or a huge yeti which appears from nowhere and chases you, including how to respond to these sudden events.

Finally, you have to demonstrate that you have indeed reached the very peak of Mount Everest. And you have to also show how you have mounted the peak in an outstanding manner, using the precise plan already defined, and not through any other means which you may have encountered along the way. For instance, if you unexpectedly meet a well-meaning Sherpa halfway up the mountain, and he has guided you to the top for a good sum of money, that is not an acceptable answer to the Deming question, unless meeting such a Sherpa was part of your plan.

In other words, the Deming examination is airtight, and the three questions give the company no place to hide.

The Deming diagnosis, 2005

Having decided on pursuing the Deming Prize, B. Muthuraman requested an initial diagnosis by the Deming team in 2005. This diagnostic study would indicate how good Tata Steel's answers were to the three Deming questions, and therefore how close the company was to the Deming Prize. The company was very confident of receiving excellent feedback on the basis of its TBEM scores over the years. Tata Steel was the undisputed champion in the group, and very proud of where it had reached.

Unfortunately, such cockiness was immediately shattered by the diagnosis. A Japanese team conducted this rigorous study and submitted a report outlining multiple areas where the company's quality approach was badly broken. It clearly highlighted that the company was not putting the customer first. It also pointed out the various inconsistencies and lack of adequate analysis in daily management. It showed how a well-knit, company-wide quality approach was sorely missing. In sum, it pointed out a harsh reality—Tata Steel may have been a quality champion within the Tata Group, but it was nowhere near winning the Deming Prize.

Dr Iwasaki of Japan, who conducted the Deming diagnosis in 2005, later asked B. Muthuraman what he felt when he received this report.

'I did the Deming diagnosis in 2005. I observe you have worked very hard since then. My question is: when you received the Deming diagnosis report three years ago, how did you feel? How did you evaluate the level of TQM in your company at that time '

B. Muthuraman responded:

> I felt disappointed. I felt hurt. We had been practising many improvement initiatives for ten to fifteen years before that. I thought we had improved. I actually thought we were good. The report came to me as a shock. But after some deep thinking for a few days, I realized I was wrong. We were not good enough. Though we had practised several improvement initiatives for many years, they were disjointed. We did not have an overall integrated philosophy.

The frog in the well had just discovered the world outside.

Actions, more actions and improvement

Deming had thrown down the gauntlet; Tata Steel decided to respond.

Muthuraman and his men of steel studied the negative

feedback from Deming. They then made investment decisions that put quality and customer requirements first. A vigorous effort was undertaken to create this mindset across Tata Steel, where every employee understood that the next process is his key customer. The management began demanding more data and more tools to analyse it. Process discipline became sacrosanct, everywhere. Every key team member was trained and retrained in the principles of TQM. Muthuraman himself, in an effort to gain further insight in this area, read up virtually every book on Toyota, which is an acknowledged master in this field.

At the end of three years of back-breaking effort, Tata Steel knew it had improved significantly. Of course, no one knew if these improvements were enough to win the Deming Prize. But since there was visible progress, Muthuraman and his team decided to invite the Deming examiners back in 2008, three years after the initial diagnosis that had set the cat among the pigeons.

Deming examination, 2008

The Deming examination is a fifteen-day high-pressure event. Over fifteen Japanese examiners, including Dr Iwasaki, visited Tata Steel's facilities in September 2008. They included people with strong academic and industrial backgrounds.

Due to the size of the company there were six individual examination units: the raw materials division; the coke, sinter and iron division; the long products division; the flat products division; the shared services division; and, finally, the corporate unit, which was a grouping of all the corporate departments. In addition to these six divisional applications, thirty-eight departmental applications had to be submitted. More than seventy individual cases of significant improvement were prepared to vividly demonstrate the TQM challenge that Tata Steel had overcome.

The examiners asked questions at every level; they met hundreds of employees across the organization. They sought working documents, process flow charts, business plans, improvement metrics and measures—in short, everything required to assess answers to the three Deming questions. Mountains of data were submitted, and they had to speak louder than words.

The executive session

The final part of the Deming examination is the executive session, where the Japanese examiners directly ask questions of the top leadership team. This tests the understanding and involvement of the managing director and other senior leaders in building the answers to the three big questions. It is perhaps the final touchstone, where examiners look for that undefinable X factor that is necessary to win the big prize.

This session was held in Tata Steel on 5 September 2008. The Tata Steel management included Managing Director B. Muthuraman, Chief Operating Officer Hemant Nerurkar and Vice-President in charge of TQM and Flat Products Anand Sen. Other members of the senior leadership team were also present.

While the entire session is too long to reproduce here, the following questions and answers provide a flavour of the philosophy and the detail that the examiners were looking for. They also bring to life the extreme clarity of thought in the senior leadership team of Tata Steel. These were transcribed by Muthuraman and team immediately after the session concluded, since the Deming examiners do not permit the use of recording devices.

Data for decision-making

Deming Examiner: You have a good highway, and as a company you are speeding up fast. How are you sure that you have not forgotten anything and that you have to go back home to fetch it? In other words, how do you ensure that you have all the information you need?

B. Muthuraman: We have robust processes, people are fully involved and we believe we have all the basic data required to take the right decisions each time. So we don't have to go back home.

Anand Sen: We have a systematic approach to ensure relevant information is always available for decision-making. We have tried to build learning systems. For example, we have built automation levels 1, 2 and 3. These are systems that learn from past events and are given options for future situations. In IT we built the basic platform with SAP, on top of that we installed the twelve system for analysis, and topped that with the managerial system of consensus-building process. More recently, we have used the TQM tool of TOC (Theory of Constraints) measurements to improve our decision-making.

Challenges in implementing total quality management (TQM)

Deming Examiner: What have you found most difficult to achieve? What was your biggest challenge in implementing TQM?

Muthuraman: We are in one of the most economically backward states of India. When our employees come inside our works, they have to 'take off one hat' and 'put on another hat'. Such is the ambience here. In this ambience, to get our employees to think of TQM, think world class—that was the biggest challenge.

Standardization, improvement and innovation

Muthuraman [responding to a request by examiners for an introductory summary submission]: In every organization, there needs to be a balance between standardization, improvement and innovation. All three are necessary, important and need to be present in a balanced manner.

People are the most important vehicle through which this balance can be achieved. To have a balanced presence of these three elements, you need to have people who are energized, enthused, empowered and happy. It is the management's job to get these traits and attributes in the people of the organization.

What will you do if you fail?

Deming Examiner: I came for the 2005 Deming diagnosis. I am impressed by the progress since then. You will know your scores shortly. But what will you do if you fail?

Muthuraman: I will be very disappointed. I want to tell you a story. There was a king who invaded India to acquire land and temples. He came and he failed. He came a second time and he failed again. He came a third time, a fourth time, a fifth time. He failed. He failed sixteen times. On his seventeenth attempt, he succeeded.

I will think like him. For me, preparing for the Deming examination is important. Passing the Deming examination is very important. But the most important of all, for me, is to continue to improve and innovate. And Deming has shown us the way.

The Deming Prize awards ceremony

The Deming examiner's question on what Tata Steel would do if it failed eventually turned out to be academic. Soon after this executive session, the Deming examination ended. A few weeks later, Muthuraman received the phone call informing him of Tata Steel's victory. The company celebrated in style, sweets were distributed as per Indian tradition and Muthuraman cut a big chocolate cake in the TQM team's office.

On 12 November 2008, at a special ceremony in Tokyo, Muthuraman represented Tata Steel and received the Deming Prize. The Indian national flag was prominent on the dais that day, which made many people at Tata Steel very proud—some even wept with joy.

Muthuraman spoke on that occasion. After speaking about his joy in becoming the only steel company outside Japan to win the Deming Prize, he went on to say:

> I began to realize that it is not because we are perfect that we are getting the Deming Prize. It is because we have taken the first steps, the first firm and sure steps towards the quality movement, and because a large number of people in the entire organization are involved in that movement, that we are being given this prestigious award.
>
> Our efforts to challenge the Deming Prize, and the questions that the Deming examiners asked us made us humble and made us realize we now have a tool and a system with which we can improve everything we do, on a continuous and predictable basis.

Accompanying Muthuraman to the awards ceremony was Raghunath Pandey, president of the employees' union of Tata Steel. There could be no better tribute to the fact that this was a grand prize earned by the 35,000 employees of the company, working together. When asked whether taking the union president along to receive the award is a rare gesture, Muthuraman says it is neither a rare gesture nor should it be one. He goes on to say:

> In the long and rich history of Tata Steel, the employees' union and the management have always worked together, journeyed together and reaped success together. The power of people is great. We need to understand this, and we need to make people realize their potential. This is the most difficult journey in any organization, but is central to its sustained success.

Life after Deming

Since then the company has successfully acquired the British steel giant, Corus, now renamed Tata Steel Europe. Economic volatility in Europe and India has posed fresh questions. Commodity price swings are more pronounced than they were in the past, introducing tremendous uncertainty into the steel manufacturing industry.

Notwithstanding these business challenges Tata Steel has now applied for the Deming Grand Prize, which is the highest Deming honour.* Companies can apply for this award three years after winning the Deming Prize if they have taken yet another big leap. Tata Steel believes that it has.

---

*At the time of going to the printers, it was announced on 9 October 2012 that Tata Steel has been awarded the Deming Grand Prize 2012. It became the first integrated steel company to win this accolade. The Deming Grand Prize is the highest honour in quality awarded to companies for excellence in TQM, and is given by the Japanese Union of Scientists and Engineers (JUSE).

Ratan Tata was once asked to name a company in the Tata Group that could act as a role model. He named Tata Steel, saying, 'Tata Steel has many of the attributes of the model company, though not all of them.'

I am positive that Tata Steel would have noted this remark, systematically identified which aspects of greatness it does not possess, and quietly begun working towards building these attributes for itself!

Epilogue

One Day in Kolkata

A memorable occasion

On 31 August, 2012, Ratan Tata chaired and addressed the Annual General Meeting (AGM) of Tata Global Beverages Limited, at the elegant Oberoi Grand Hotel in Kolkata. This was a memorable day, because it was the last AGM he was addressing as chairman, before his scheduled retirement at the end of the year. Also present at the meeting were R.K. Krishna Kumar, who has appeared earlier in this book as the architect of the Tetley acquisition, and Cyrus Mistry, selected earlier in the year to succeed Ratan Tata as chairman of Tata Sons.

The AGM of Tata Global Beverages has traditionally been held in Kolkata, where the registered office of the company is located. The local newspapers had already headlined Ratan Tata's arrival in the city. The *Telegraph* carried a beautiful black-and-white photograph showing him in a car, wearing the buttoned down collared shirt he is so fond of. Most of the media reports spoke about him bidding farewell to the city of joy.

This was also a memorable occasion for me, because I had

the unique privilege of being seated on the dais with Ratan Tata and other directors. I had recently been appointed the managing director of Tata Global Beverages. From this vantage position, I could see the large audience of over a thousand people, comprising shareholders, employees of the company and members of the media. They were waiting to hear Ratan Tata, and many of them were also eager to speak.

What did they speak about? There were questions about and comments on several areas of the Tata beverages business, including growth plans and profit margins. These are routine matters in any company's annual general meeting. A string of speakers rose to convey lavish praise and thanks to Ratan Tata, for everything he had done, and for the splendid leadership he had provided. These were emotional moments for everyone in the large hall.

Remarkably, many subjects that were highlighted and discussed that morning had little to do with the beverages business, but everything to do with the Tata Way. As I listened, these topics once again highlighted to me what makes the Tata Group such an inspiring institution.

World-class cancer management and care

Several speakers came to the podium to appreciate the Tata Medical Centre, which had recently been established in Kolkata. With a mission of providing world-class cancer management and care to all sections of society, this state-of-the-art hospital was also straight from the heart. The centre was yet another philanthropic initiative by the Tata Group, and it had already made a big impact in Kolkata and the north-east.

T.P. Goel, a participant in the meeting, walked up and spoke with a quiver in his voice, as he mentioned what a boon the medical centre had been. He said that his daughter-in-law had been treated in the hospital, and had obtained the best possible treatment. He spoke with happiness that she was now recovering well. He then went on to add that not only was the treatment excellent but the food served in the hospital was also very affordable!

Ratan Tata thanked him for his observations and recalled how the hospital had its genesis in discussions that had been held in that very room. He said that a large number of cancer patients from the eastern and north-eastern region of the country had to earlier travel all the way to Mumbai for treatment. Hence the Tata Group had felt that Kolkata needed a modern hospital that could help deal with the ravaging disease. Later that afternoon, he also visited the hospital and addressed its staff members. Here was an institution that Kolkata could derive strength from, and be proud of.

Sir, I said no

A young shareholder, Adarsh, rose to speak about how the Tata Group and Ratan Tata were an inspiration to him for the principled conduct of business. He narrated how a tax officer had demanded a bribe from him to provide a statutory approval required in his business. He went on to say:

'Sir, I was inspired by you, and I refused to pay the bribe. Instead, I chose to appoint a lawyer to argue my case and obtain the approval legally. We call you Guruji; we are inspired by you. So when I read in newspapers that you were in town today, I dropped everything else and came here, because I just wanted to say a grateful thanks to you.'

The young man then walked up to Ratan Tata with pride, shook his hand and melted away into the crowd.

Will the Tata Group invest in West Bengal?

This was a question on many lips that morning, particularly since the Tata Group had been forced to relocate its small car plant from Singur in West Bengal a few years ago, after protests led by the political leader Mamata Banerjee. This pioneering venture had since been shifted to the state of Gujarat, which had welcomed it with open arms.

Ratan Tata responded that the Tata Group would continue to promote pioneering ventures. It would certainly support future investments in West Bengal, should such opportunities present themselves. The Tatas had tried to bring a car manufacturing facility here, he added, the people had always been warm and friendly, but differences at a political level had come in the way. He then went on to say that the Singur matter did not anger him but only created a sense of sadness. He chose not to comment on the specific issues at hand, since the matter is subjudice. However, the Tata Group would fully respect decisions of the law. One day, he hoped, Tata Motors would be welcomed back to West Bengal.

There were, however, unspoken questions that lingered in the room. Could the Singur story have been handled differently by the Tatas? Would history judge that the group's approach had been less than perfect? Could there have been a happier ending, and indeed, could one be crafted now? What were the important lessons for the future?

Coffee at Starbucks, water from the Himalayas

The pioneering spirit of the Tata Group came to the fore once again when some shareholders spoke about Tata Starbucks, a joint venture company that had been established recently to set up cafes in India. Stores bearing the façade 'Starbucks, a

Tata alliance' would soon appear across all major Indian cities. The stores would locally source roasted coffee beans from Tata Coffee Limited for all its espressos. This made the venture unique, since such local sourcing was not normally pursued by the Starbucks Coffee Company in other parts of the world.

Other shareholders spoke of Himalayan water, the single-origin premium brand of water marketed by Tata Global Beverages. Fed by an underground Himalayan acquifier, this was a unique and natural brand of water that had the potential to establish itself as a water of choice across the world. It was already making good inroads into Indian cities, as it established a large new premium segment for bottled water in the country.

Ratan Tata briefly touched upon how both these ventures were breaking new ground. Tata Global Beverages, which had been a relatively small Indian tea company before its acquisition of Tetley, was now chasing big ambitions in natural beverages such as coffee and water.

Pioneering, Purposive, Principled, not Perfect

I was quite amazed that all the four Ps that mark out the Tata Way were reflected by these speakers, in the course of a single meeting lasting just a few hours.

Himalayan water and Tata Starbucks are pioneering initiatives. The Tata Medical Centre is certainly purposive. The youngster who did not give a bribe was inspired by the principled character of the Tatas. The Singur episode throws up questions of whether the company's approach here was less than perfect, and from this there will certainly emerge some lessons for the future.

These tales from one day in Kolkata, and the stories that you have read in the earlier chapters of this book, make the point that the Tata Way is a path that has been well paved for this timeless institution over the more than 150 years of its existence. But it is also a path that has to be constantly nurtured and watered, so that it is always borne in mind and consistently used. That is the happy privilege and sacred responsibility of the leaders and all the people of Tata, also called Tata *Log*.